More Praise for *Portfolio First Aid*

"The real benefit of *Portfolio First Aid* is that the two authors avoid providing band-aid solutions for ailing portfolios. They offer comprehensive and sensible insights to breathe new life and health into any investor's financial plan."
  Peter Bailey, President, Raymond James Ltd.

"For all investors who want to know and understand the investment process, this book is essential. *Portfolio First Aid* is a masterly guide to both new and experienced investors because the process is always in a state of change. The wisdom and experience of the two authors is presented in a manner which is clearly understandable."
  C. Warren Goldring, Chairman of the Board, AGF Management Limited

"A useful and entertaining tour of the investment world that hits all the significant ports of call. Written by two veteran financial advisors in a vividly descriptive fashion, it offers sage advice enhanced by personal anecdotes and humor. This book will help investors avoid costly mistakes and develop a strategy that can withstand the drama of shifting market moods."
  Jade Hemeon, Financial Writer

"*Portfolio First Aid* offers just what investors need—a deep understanding of financial markets, the right tools to nurture and grow investment assets, and a good dose of tender loving care in its purest form: wisdom, distilled from the co-authors' long investment experience. All of this is put together in a readable style that is accessible and astute. Investors have rarely been treated so well."
  Mark Mullins, Ph.D., Former Chief Economist, Midland Walwyn Capital Inc.

"*Portfolio First Aid* is a prescription that will aid all investors from the sophisticated to the novice. This book covers all aspects of investing...it is extremely comprehensive while being an entertaining read."
  Robert Schultz, Chairman, Rockwater Capital, Former Chief Executive Officer, Merrill Lynch Canada and Midland Walwyn

PORTFOLIO

FIR$T AID

PORTFOLIO

FIR$T AID

EXPERT ADVICE FOR HEALTHIER INVESTING

Michael Graham, Ph.D. & Bryan Snelson

John Wiley & Sons Canada, Ltd.

Library and Archives Canada Cataloguing in Publication Data

Graham, Michael
     Portfolio first aid: expert advice for healthier investing / Michael Graham, Bryan Snelson.

Includes index.
ISBN-13 978-470-83647-7
ISBN-10 0-470-83647-4

1. Investments. 2. Portfolio management. 3. Finance, Personal.
I.   Graham, Michael II. Title.

HG179.S527 2005   332.6   C2005-902777-0

Production Credits:
Cover design: Ian Koo
Interior text design: Natalia Burobina
Printer: Transcontinental

John Wiley & Sons Canada, Ltd.
6045 Freemont Blvd.
Mississauga, Ontario
L5R 4J3

Printed in Canada

10 9 8 7 6 5 4 3 2 1

Michael Graham

Michael dedicates *Portfolio First Aid* to the investors and their advisors from all walks of life who have read his articles and attended his presentations over forty years: You have no idea what your support and encouragement have meant to me—and what an opportune way this is to be able to record my heartfelt thanks.

Bryan Snelson

To my wife Cathy and my daughters Laura and Sydney whose patience, encouragement and love means more to me than they will ever know. To my clients who have placed their trust in me and keep me gainfully employed. To the two unsung heroes whose professionalism and friendship make coming to work everyday a pleasure and who consistently manage to make me appear to be much smarter than I actually am; Linda Stragliotto and Carrie Hathaway. To all of you *Portfolio First Aid* is gratefully dedicated.

Contents

Preface

Portfolio First Aid is a book we have both long wanted to write, perhaps for different reasons but always with the same common goal.

Michael already has two publications to his name; a doctoral dissertation undertaken at the London School of Economics before Canada came into his life, and successfully completed in January 1964; and a Corporate Background Report on the Canada Development Corporation for the Royal Commission on Corporate Concentration published in January 1976. There is also his 214 pages of bound testimony in *Brascan Limited against Edper Equities Ltd.* "written" in a New York courtroom in May 1979. Hundreds of research studies, articles and papers add to his extensive bibliography. But until now never the book on investing he has often thought of writing, and that many friends have just has often asked why he hasn't.

Bryan's passion for the cut and thrust of free enterprise was ignited during his early twenties when he started a small business, toiling day and night until it flourished. He has long been drawn to the stories of the men and women who, through their ingenuity and sheer will, have helped to shape nations and change the world. His passion for and fascination with enterprise were fulfilled when he sold his business and entered the world of bulls and bears. Having the opportunity to write this book with a man who has been a pivotal figure in his professional life is the culmination of a long held dream for Bryan.

Portfolio First Aid is the result of two careers that collectively represent more than half a century of hard work with thousands of families from all walks of life. It is our hope that you will prosper from reading of both the good and unfortunate experiences of the investors with whom we have had the opportunity to meet. Our aim is to share the collective experience we have gained over the years: The highs, the lows, what we have learnt and what investing can come to mean if approached with care and precision. Above all, we want to introduce you to a very necessary process that will help you to remain focused so that you can make better, and more consistent investment decisions, which of course should lead to better and more consistent results.

There is little that pleases us more than when someone comments on how much they learned from our presentations, writings and broadcasts. Too often, however, the comments are tinged with regret: "If I only knew then what you told us now." and "What can I do to stop my portfolio from bleeding more red ink?" were common refrains from the people who came to us for help during and after the savage bear market of 2000-2002.

There is nothing worse than having to inform an investor that his or her hard-earned savings has been badly mauled—sometimes irreparably. What a shame that investors and their advisors became so badly and suspiciously separated, and the investing public lost so much confidence in what should be a rewarding process.

The sad part is that so much of what went awry needn't have happened. It is for this reason that *Portfolio First Aid* is aimed at advisors as much as it is at individual investors.

This said, at no point do we intend to replace the considerable expertise that already exists in an industry that is more professional than ever before. Nor do we wish *Portfolio First Aid* to compete with the efforts of dedicated, top-flight professionals who are far better equipped than we are—or may ever be. Instead, our intent is to help you to not only make the most of the money you have, but at the same time to preserve your undoubtedly hard-earned wealth and make it grow the way you would want—and need.

To know more about the essentials of investing, to learn from past experience, to capture the excitement of an increasingly globalized world in which investors could become king and a streamlined, "new-look" Canada enters a thrilling investment era—these are the goals of the three-section "conversation" to follow.

If *Portfolio First Aid* leaves you with an improved and excited understanding of what contemporary investing should be all about, this labour of love will have been all the more worthwhile.

Michael Graham & Bryan Snelson
Summer 2005

Acknowledgements

Many people are referred to in this work. Some expressly allowed us to use their names. Then there are the many others without whose views, expert knowledge and source material *Portfolio First Aid* and its central message would hardly have been possible. We are most grateful to them all.

In addition, there are those who have lived and breathed *Portfolio First Aid* with us through its various stages, some right from the beginning, and without whose help and encouragement we couldn't have done it.

Bryan particularly wishes to thank Brad Shoemaker who was there at the genesis of *Portfolio First Aid*. Brad's enduring wisdom, friendly counsel and just plain old friendship have helped to make the sometimes very long hours seem to fly by. Many thanks as well to Peter Kahnert for helping to open more doors of opportunity for Bryan over the years than he can count. Gabor Szekely and Ken Beck are two men to whom Bryan extends a heartfelt and long overdue thanks for their guidance and encouragement in getting him started in the investment industry.

Portfolio First Aid never would have taken shape if it had not been for the inspiration of countless listeners to JAZZ FM91 in Toronto. Thank you for listening and for your input.

Michael could not have coped without the untiring help of Edna Billsborough, his irreplaceable, long-time personal assistant. His wife Nancy was another he could constantly lean on for help in the choice of the right words and ideas, not to forget her considerable editing and text-reading skills and her understanding encouragement. Their children Julia, Richard and Hugh have known about "the book" all along, and Michael also wishes to thank them for cheering him on. Rena LePage of VCG Creative Imaging willingly provided and topped up many of the slides she has made for Michael over the years. Finally, there are Michael's partners —Rob Richards, Rupel Ruparelia and Richard Tattersall—at Heathbridge Capital Management Ltd. who he thanks for their understanding support.

Both of us are indebted to John Hirst for his experienced and wise counsel in the lead-up stage to *Portfolio First Aid*. In addition, we are extremely grateful to Terry Palmer of Wiley Canada for her constant reassurance that we could do it and, once the manuscript was handed to them, to Karen Milner and her team for steering us so ably to the finish line.

We wish space permitted mention of all the others whose comments, encouragement and ideas contributed to *Portfolio First Aid* in one way or the other. You know who you are, we know who you are, and we are immensely grateful.

Bryan Snelson & Michael Graham
Summer 2005

PART ONE

DIAGNOSIS

CHAPTER 1

Irrational Exuberance and the Lessons Learned

If there were a single impetus for *Portfolio First Aid* it was the savage bear market of 2000–2002. A bear market like few others exposed any and all weaknesses in the portfolios of investors ranging from the novice through to seasoned professionals. The speed and ferocity of that historic market downturn caught most investors ill prepared, in many instances resulting in delayed retirement plans and lifestyle changes. From an advisor's point of view, there is nothing worse than having to tell well-intentioned investors that their portfolio has been pounded beyond recognition. The purpose of this book is to serve as a guide on how to begin the often-necessary healing process and to offer counsel on practical steps to reduce the risk of such serious financial injury in the future.

From maximum pessimism to maximum optimism and back again to maximum pessimism; from pain to euphoria and back to pain; from fear to greed and back to fear. And accompanying all of these mood swings, irrational negativity *and* irrational exuberance. The years 1982 to 2002 contained many lessons, even for hardened investment professional like ourselves, the primary lesson being that, to borrow a line from the Boy Scouts, we should always *be prepared*.

Market fluctuations are a fact of life for all investors, much like winds buffeting a tall building. The challenge for us as investors is to ensure that our portfolios have adequate structural integrity to withstand the continuous strains brought about by the daily push and pull of the world's financial markets. For the millions of investors who suffered through the 2000–2002 bear market, the seeds of their despair were sown long before the markets swooned. The financial bloodshed that drove us to write *Portfolio First Aid* was, admittedly in some instances, utterly unavoidable. In our experience, though, the damage could have been substantially mitigated through careful planning, vigilance and discipline long before trouble appeared on the horizon. To illustrate this point, we need to examine what has happened in the past for a glimpse of what may occur in the future. Among the world's financial markets, history does tend to repeat itself, validating that famous phrase which warned that those who fail to learn from the lessons of the past are doomed to repeat it.

There couldn't be a better starting point than the summer of 1982 to illustrate what we mean and what this book is all about.

In that fear-filled summer, little did investors or investment professionals realize that we were witnessing the birth of an 18-year bull market that was to spawn countless fortunes, make America approximately 15 times richer (and Canada about four times richer) and inspire millions of new, first-time investors.

Like all bull markets, the great bull market of 1982–2000 was born in the eye of a storm—in this case, a protracted storm that will never be forgotten by those, like Michael, who lived through it. In retrospect, the birthing process of that great bull market couldn't have been more tortuous.

THE SUMMER OF DISCONTENT

Pessimism was rampant in the summer of 1982. Economies were gripped by an unusually savage recession, the stock markets were the pits and investors everywhere were in the depths of despair. Joe Granville, a self-proclaimed investment guru with a large following, was warning all and sundry that this was the last chance to get out. So bleak was the overall mood that there were even days when optimists like Michael wondered whether Chicken Little might indeed be right. If ever there were a time when successful investing required *fortitude* (one of Sir John Templeton's favourite words), the summer of 1982 was it.

It was only years later, with the benefit of hindsight, that one could look back and see the accompanying emergence of a glittering new era and with it the greatest bull market of our lifetime, maybe of all time.

That summer, to say that stocks and related equity investments had fallen from favour would be an understatement. The bellwether Dow Jones Industrial

Average, which had first broken the psychologically important 1,000 barrier in early 1966, and did so again briefly in early 1973, was drifting listlessly down in the mid-700 range. This was some 20 to 25% below its level of *16 years* before. To rub salt in investor wounds, the Dow had been mired in a narrow trading range for the better part of the previous 10 years.

An entire generation of investors who had bought their first stocks in the mid- to late 1960s, when the stock market indexes were in a tight race with Apollo astronauts to reach the moon, began experiencing moods of self-doubt. As events transpired, buy-and-hold investors who had committed their savings to equities of the type represented by the broad-market Standard & Poor's 500 index were going to have nothing to show for their patience for the next several years. Few investors—especially of that new generation—had that kind of persistence. All the while, the markets were working in their wondrous, self-adjusting ways.

Offshore capital that first made its way into the bond market was beginning to find scores of North American companies trading at tempting, fire-sale prices. Something was stirring deep within the markets, yet come the summer of 1982 the default position of most investors had made them leery of yet another bear trap. On August 23, the investment weekly *Barron's* had the tongue-in-cheek temerity to put a bull on its cover and ask, "Is this bull for real?" The reaction of many subscribers was openly hostile.

THE ICON SPEAKS

During that same summer, on Louis Rukeyser's *Wall Street Week*, Sir John Templeton predicted that an American child being born at that time would never be able to buy stocks more cheaply in his or her lifetime. At the same time, Sir John made another bold prediction: The Dow would reach 3,000 within five years. His logic? Corporate earnings would double over this period, as would price-earnings ratios, which had been cut in half from a decade earlier. Two times two gave a factor of four with which to multiply a Dow in the 750–770 range for a breathtaking target of 3,000. Beautifully simple and logical, except no one believed him!

The Dow did eventually reach 3,000 in the spring of 1991, meaning Sir John had missed out by more than four years. Nevertheless, what prescience this investment icon showed in the depths of the despairing summer of 1982, and how worthwhile it would have been to heed his sage advice of the time.

THE TIDE BEGINS TO TURN—BUT DOUBTS REMAIN

In mid-August 1982, seemingly without warning, the tide began to turn. With increasing regularity, more and more significant up-days began to appear on swelling trading volumes.

Nevertheless, suspicion was rife. Michael remembers attending a meeting of investment industry professionals that concluded it was all a bear trap to lull the unwary, and that one should be selling on this unexpected—and unwarranted—strength.

Instead, what was underway was a new bull market that was to take the Dow to over 11,000 by the end of the century—not straight up, mind you, and not without some nerve-testing traumas en route. Regardless, the pendulum had begun swinging from irrational fear to irrational optimism, and to the inevitable need for another major cataclysmic shakeout that would eventually bring the great bull market born in the summer of 1982 to an end in the spring of 2000.

By the mid-1980s all of the previous pain and loss was forgiven and forgotten (or so it seemed). The North American investing public's love affair with stocks was once again in full bloom.

GREED IS GOOD

The 1980s, the era of the junk bond and its offspring, the leveraged buyout, also saw the markets driven higher by LBO (leveraged buy out) leviathans like T. Boone Pickens, Carl Icahn and Alan Bond on the prowl for their next seductive takeover target. The era was personified by the character of Gordon Gekko, played by Michael Douglas in the Oliver Stone film *Wall Street*. For many who saw the film, the mid- to late 1980s leveraged buyout boom was captured in its essence when Douglas's character, standing in a classic gunslinger pose, declared that "greed is good."

The appetite for stock investing among individuals and institutions was growing increasingly ravenous. It was again becoming all too easy to make money in the stock markets. Standards began slipping, but who cared? The inevitable result was a dramatic increase in share prices, but also markets that were once again setting up for a fall.

DISTANT EARLY WARNING

In late August 1987, the Dow Jones Industrial Average reached an all-time peak of 2,722. At that point its 30 component stocks were priced at a 20 times average price-to-earnings multiple, a level last seen at the Dow's old peak of 14 years earlier. For the first time since the early 1980s, more Wall Street research analysts were raising their estimates of corporate earnings than lowering them. For those who thought about it, there were lots of fresh warning signs on the wall.

In the midst of this euphoria there were some who had been tracking the market's ebb and flow for long enough to recognize a familiar pattern emerging. One was Canadian-born Harvard economist John Kenneth Galbraith, who, writing in the *Atlantic Monthly*, reported a "speculative buildup" taking shape. Despite his impeccable credentials, and like Sir John Templeton before him, Galbraith was roundly dismissed. His detractors pointed to the benefits bestowed upon corporate earnings by the spate of company restructurings. High price-to-earnings multiples, it was argued, could be justified as a by-product of greater degrees of cost control and burgeoning global economic growth. Sounds familiar, doesn't it?

By October, the weather certainly seemed to be foreshadowing strange days ahead when London was unexpectedly blasted by its first hurricane since 1703. Never one to be superstitious, Michael, in London on a business trip, couldn't help but wonder if the fickle English weather had a hand in the North American stock markets' biggest swan dive since the great crash of 1929.

BLACK MONDAY: OCTOBER 19, 1987

It is not unusual for us to remember in vivid detail where we were and precisely what we were doing at certain dramatic moments of our modern history. Events like the Kennedy assassination in November 1963, Paul Henderson's winning goal in the 1972 Canada Cup Series and September 11, 2001, are days seared into the collective consciousness. For anyone who had money in the markets at the time, Monday, October 19, 1987 will always rank as such a day.

Michael, by then back from his business trip where the London Stock Exchange had been effectively closed the preceding Friday because few, if any, could get to work in a blacked-out London, had touched base with Merrill Lynch colleagues over the weekend. The consensus was that the previous week's selling had been overdone, and that we should recommend to clients that they buy. On Monday morning, October 19, these thoughts were tempered by the news that the London Stock Exchange was experiencing one of its biggest sell-offs in history—the result of all those carry-over sell orders from the previous Friday. At noon the Dow was down another hundred points or so, but the thought was that it might be bottoming.

On this note, Michael set off to the Toronto airport for his flight to Winnipeg and then on to Brandon, where he was to speak at an investment seminar that same evening. At the Winnipeg airport, a call to Toronto to check the market close brought the staggering news that the Dow had closed down 508 points, at 1,738. The drive to Brandon was sobering to say the least. How does one give a presentation on the merits of investing after a 23% single-day decline, the largest in history? By reiterating the golden rules of balance and diversification (that same day the bond market had soared), by sticking to one's beliefs and by being *very* brave!

The next day found Michael back in Winnipeg and the free-fall continuing. It isn't often that Michael loses his nerve, but that day he could stand it no longer and had to get out of the Merrill Lynch office and go walking; he remembers strolling along Broadway in bright October sunshine. On returning to the office he found that freshly minted Federal Reserve Board Chairman Alan Greenspan had reassured investors the Fed would not stand idly by and would be providing all the liquidity the markets and economy would need. Institutional investors began buying in earnest; the markets soared and the immediate crisis was over.

By day's end there had been a massive intra-day rally, and the Dow ended up 102 points. Investors trained to "buy on dips" had rushed back into the market, holding firm in beliefs that had become investment orthodox practice over the preceding five years.

As the months following the market crash rolled by and the global economy continued to expand, barely missing a beat, the sting of the market's decline faded from investors' collective psyche and the legend of the bull market took on greater proportions. Before long, investors rekindled their love affair with stocks, either directly or via what was becoming a burgeoning array of mutual funds. Today, Black Monday of October 1987 is but a blip on stock market charts and screens. It should also be a reminder of the bargain-basement opportunities that were presented to those who had properly positioned portfolios and the investment wherewithal to take advantage, and who could keep their heads when all around were losing theirs.

THE ROARING '90S: CONNECTIVITY AND CAPITALISM

For many of today's investors, their first taste of the markets came during the 1990s, which like the decade that preceded it began with economic recession. Though much of the story of the 1990s was about connectivity via the rise of the Internet, and capitalism thanks to the wave of entrepreneurial activity brought about by the new information age, a third C—the Cold War (as in the end thereof)—finished out the 1980s and ushered in the 1990s. Soviet Premier Mikhail Gorbachev's programs of *glasnost* and *perestroika*, together with increasing degrees of pressure from the likes of U.S. President Ronald Reagan, British Prime Minister Margaret Thatcher and even Pope John Paul II, opened a crack in the vast Soviet empire. On November 9, 1989, the Berlin Wall fell, East Germans were reunited with West Germans. The Cold War was over.

THE PEACE DIVIDEND

A period of substantial economic growth was about to begin, thanks in part to what became known as "the Peace Dividend." Before this dividend could begin being paid, though, another war would have to be won (the Persian Gulf War) and a recession overcome.

As had happened 10 years before, the early 1990s threatened to sideline the bull market with another dose of cripplingly high interest rates. While the rate increases of 1990–1991 were not on the same scale as the stagflation-busting rate increases of 1981–1982, there was plenty of drama nonetheless. Many of the highly leveraged buyout kings of the 1980s, from Robert Campeau to Carl Icahn, were brought to their knees by a rapid increase in lending rates orchestrated to slay inflation. Bankruptcies rose and markets swooned midway through 1990 as the North American economy slipped into recession. Thereafter, inflation began settling back down, leading interest rates to begin to subside to single digits in Canada by February of 1991 (the bank rate had been at more than 13% a year earlier). However, it didn't stop there, and to the surprise of many, particularly GIC and bond investors, interest rates declined with increasing velocity through 1992 and 1993 before the Bank of Canada rate reached a cycle low of 3.88% in January 1994.

THE GIC REFUGEE

Accompanying this decline in interest rates, a new breed of investor was being born—the GIC refugee. In a country accustomed to receiving double-digit rates of interest on their term deposits, millions of Canadians were startled at the greatly diminished renewal rates offered. Exasperated, legions of these "refugees" began casting covetous glances at the stock markets. While interest rates kept falling, stocks soared and mutual fund companies wasted no expense to highlight the double-digit rates of return of which their funds were capable, in the same manner in which a proud parent brags about their children at a family picnic.

All too suddenly the Dow began a spectacular climb through one thousand-point threshold after another—3,000 in April 1991, 4,000 in February 1995, 5,000 in November 1995, 6,000 in October 1996, 7,000 in February 1997 and 8,000 in July 1997.

BLACK MONDAY REDUX

Inevitably, just as had happened 10 years earlier, there came a need for this new-found exuberance to be cooled, and for "heady" and overly expectant (dare we say greedy) investors to once again be brought down to earth. The stage was being set for yet another October Black Monday and another 500-point single-day decline, this time on October 27, 1997, when the Dow crashed by 554 points to close at 7,161. However, rather than 23%, this decline was *only* 7%.

Michael was once again in London, and this time opted for an evening of Noel Coward theatre instead of a long walk to calm his nerves. Rather than Alan Greenspan, it was the renowned investment strategist Abby Joseph Cohen who was providing reassurance that the markets were going to be okay when Michael got back to his hotel room.

That reversal was quickly recouped, and equities were soon launched into the final and most powerful leg of the great bull market. It was preceded by Alan Greenspan's now famous late 1996 "irrational exuberance" speech in which the United States' central banker wondered aloud if investors weren't getting a little ahead of themselves regarding expectations on the future of the stock market. New thresholds were ticked off in rapid order—9,000 in April 1998, 10,000 in March 1999 and finally 11,000 in May 1999.

Y2K

What was to prove the ultimate peak of the great bull market of 1982–2000, and the genesis of this book, also coincided with the new millennium and its associated Y2K worries. However, when the lights stayed on and computerized systems everywhere made the change without a hitch at midnight on Friday, December 31, 1999, high-flying tech stocks took off afresh, and the markets were to have a final bout of irrational exuberance. Michael remembers the market capitalization of Cisco approaching U.S.$500 billion, at which level this single company was valued at some five times the GDP of his native South Africa. Madness like this couldn't last—and it didn't.

The rally in the spring of 2000 didn't exceed the Dow's peak of the previous year. With the benefit of hindsight it can now be said that this was a clear-cut sign that the bull market was running out of steam. What was to follow couldn't have been more excruciatingly painful.

ENTER THE BEAR

Whereas bull markets are born in the depths of pain and despair, bear markets tiptoe in at the heights of euphoria. However, few could have appreciated the gauntlet of troubles that was to lie ahead over the next three years: the bursting of that grossly inflated tech bubble (the biggest speculative bubble in history); the horrors of September 11, 2001; growing corporate malfeasance and an accompanying breakdown in trust (that most sacred of investment ingredients); the Iraq war and its aftermath; mounting fiscal deficits; proliferating government and consumer debt; and the collapse of the once-mighty U.S. dollar.

Investors found themselves pitchforked into a savage bear market rather than a glorious new millennium—a brand new experience for a whole generation of beginner investors, and a painful reminder for the ill-prepared to always be prepared.

Typically, bear markets average 15 months and take the market back down 30%. The bear market that ushered in the new millennium was to last 30 months and bring a correction that was closer to 50%. Rather than a healthy restorative process, this bear market subjected investors to what could well have been *the* perfect stock market storm, in which almost every portfolio lost value and those not properly structured were blown clean over—a great many never to return.

In due course, as they always do, that bear market was also to end and a new bull market to be born, once again in the depths of another icy October. However, it was only months later, when the lows of October 2002 withstood a fresh onslaught in the spring of 2003, that we knew for sure that the ferocious bear market of 2000–2002 was over.

WALLS OF WORRY

The lexicon of Wall Street is peppered with phrases meant to remind, inspire and warn, including one that *investors must always be climbing walls of worry*. Over the years of making a living in the business of advising people on how best to invest their hard-earned dollars, we've learned the hard way that if you're not sweating the details—climbing walls of worry—a cavalier attitude and a degree of carelessness can seep into the decision-making process. The results can be, and often are, costly—occasionally even lifestyle altering.

WHAT IF?

Writing in the *Wall Street Journal* more than 100 years ago, Charles Dow, that great Wall Street theorist and the originator of the Dow Jones Industrial Average, recognized those most basic elements of investor psychology: fear and greed (which we will explore in much greater detail in Chapter 3). Dow wrote that "There is always a disposition in people's minds to think that the existing conditions will be permanent. When [stock] prices are up and the country is prosperous, it is always said that while preceding booms have not lasted, this time there are unique circumstances which will make prosperity permanent."

Eighty years later, Sir John Templeton put it even more succinctly when he stated that the most expensive phrase in the language of Wall Street is "this time it's different." Sound familiar?

We'll go one step further and say that the two most *profitable* words an investor can utter are "what if." It's often been said that armies are best prepared to fight the last war, yet we know that survival on the battlefield demands extensive preparations and a willingness to adapt to changing conditions once the enemy is engaged.

Economists, academics, portfolio managers and politicians all expend tremendous amounts of time and energy trying to get a fix on where the world is heading. This is as it should be, but who hasn't heard of that guy Murphy and his law? The point is this: We live, and always have lived, in an uncertain world. For every risk there is an opportunity. Use the resources around you to plan for the future when constructing your portfolio, but remember that no one has an entirely infallible crystal ball. Always ask yourself, and your advisor for that matter, "what if...?" Circumstances change. In our world of instant communications and a 24-hour news cycle, change occurs faster than at any other time in human history.

If you've learned anything from this opening chapter's brief history lesson, it should be that change is constant and seldom occurs when expected. To embrace this fact of life in the world of investing is to take a quantum leap forward in your development as an investor.

CHAPTER 2

Self-Inflicted Wounds

The Most Common Strategic Errors Made by Investors

As we discussed in Chapter 1, memories of a market reversal fade in direct proportion to the speed and altitude of that market's advance. Not surprisingly, this also has the tendency to lead to heightened levels of bravado among investors who then begin to unwittingly take on greater degrees of risk.

In the course of our work with legions of individual investors, a number of potentially painful themes appear repeatedly. Many of these self-inflicted wounds, if left untended, can fester, growing into substantially more serious and costly problems. That's the bad news. The good news is that most if not all of the wounds we've tended to are fairly easy to treat. Should you recognize some of your own foibles nestled among those chronicled here, take comfort in the fact that you are not alone. These are injuries that are so easy to fall victim to. You certainly weren't the first, and neither will you be the last. Our message is to not give up in the face of adversity; giving up metastasizes something entirely treatable into something terminal.

In Chapter 3, our focus will shift to tactical errors, most of which involve our own basic human failings. Some of these portfolio ailments may also have a certain ring of familiarity. Once again, take heart, as we show you how to stage a complete recovery.

THE NUMBER ONE ERROR OF OMISSION: WHERE ARE THE BONDS?

Though this chapter will deal with errors of *commission*, it is not uncommon for us to review a wounded portfolio only to discover that the root problems stem from what the owner overlooked or omitted. All too often this can be as simple as a dearth of fixed-income securities and, following from this, a portfolio lacking the all-important requirement of proper balance.

During the late 1990s, in what turned out to be the last phase of the greatest bull market of the 20th century, it became fashionable to shun bonds. What had happened was that as inflation came under control, central bankers became able to bring lending rates down to levels not seen since the times of Eisenhower and Diefenbaker, which meant that bonds provided relatively poor returns in the eyes of investors who had in years past become accustomed to much more lucrative yields. The net result was that many investors felt compelled to recapture some of what they used to receive in the form of yield by entering the stock market —many indirectly via mutual funds, and many for the first time in their lives. Early successes by these investors chased away any butterflies the typical investor may have had when making his or her first investment. The sometimes substantial gains realized by these neophyte investors quickly changed the way they looked at bonds and all other fixed-income investments. Suddenly, bonds were like the contestant who wins Miss Congeniality at a beauty pageant. Equities, meanwhile, had won the swimsuit competition.

FLYING WITHOUT A NET

The tragedy is that running a portfolio without fixed-income securities is a little like the Flying Wallendas—performing without a net. In the late 1990s, starry-eyed investors were all too often trying to make apples-to-apples comparisons between bonds, which have a fixed rate of return, and equities, which were in rapid ascent. Just as often, the illogical conclusion was that having bonds in their turbo-charged growth portfolios served the same purpose as aerodynamic drag: unnecessarily slowing things down.

To stretch this tortured metaphor a little more, the reality is that having a fixed-income segment in a growth portfolio is not so much *aerodynamic drag* as having a *drag chute* on a top-fuel racer. It's understandable, and desirable, to want to achieve maximum velocity when market conditions permit. There will come a time, though, when the stock markets will falter. At that point, you will recognize the need to be able to gear down to navigate through the difficult market conditions that will inevitably get in your way.

GRANDMA'S GOT HER GAME FACE ON

It's not just the growth investor who can fail to remember the role that fixed-income investments play in a properly balanced portfolio. Investors in need of income, such as retirees, can also fall victim to the temptation of foregoing bonds in favour of a growth strategy that they think will meet their needs more easily. This is invariably the case in advanced bull market phases like the late 1990s. Early in a bull market, these self-described conservative, income-dependent investors still retain vivid memories of market downturns. We've seen time and again, however, that these memories quickly fade. As the major market averages scale new heights, the terms used to describe one's risk tolerance start to become increasingly subjective. All of a sudden, Grandma has a portfolio stuffed full of growth stocks, and she's on the phone to her broker demanding to know why Millie at the bridge club is getting more growth on her portfolio than she is.

Bryan vividly remembers his office's Christmas potluck luncheon in 1999 when the brokers gathered around the massive mahogany boardroom table, nibbling on nachos, nursing lukewarm beer and swapping stories of "irrational exuberance." Every broker had at least one story to tell of a verbal tongue-lashing from a stereotypical little old lady for failing to deliver growth that kept pace with a day-trading friend (despite asset allocations and risk tolerances geared to conservatism and income generation). Michael remembers similar examples of clients objecting loudly when he recommended cutting back on suddenly disproportionately large holdings in Nortel Networks as it kept reaching for the sky.

The stories one year later couldn't have been in more stark contrast. By December 2000, a bear market had begun taking hold in earnest, and those same Jekyll and Hyde investors were reverting to their conservative personas with a vengeance. More than this, as equity markets swooned, and Nortel's share price crashed with drama paralleled only by the ill-fated Hindenburg, many investors became paralyzed with fear. They fervently hoped that the decline was nothing more than an aberration. During the market's rise, they had been able to draw income from their portfolios without eating into their capital, thereby gaining the mistaken impression that growth investments were also suitable for income-dependent investors. The cold reality began to set in: drawing income from a portfolio that is declining in value is akin to compounding in reverse, and as a consequence, investors who are the least able to withstand a downturn suffer significantly greater harm than others. This is exactly what happened with a vengeance as the ferocious bear market of 2000–2002 took hold.

BONDS AS A BUFFER

This brings us back to the true purpose of fixed-income investments. Even for growth-seeking investors, fixed income plays the role of a buffer, smoothing out the inevitable peaks and valleys in portfolio performance and providing the liquidity to fund fresh investment when the market opportunity arises.

For the income-seeking investor, fixed-income investments, with their set maturity dates and regular interest payments, offer a degree of income and capital preservation commensurate with the degree of credit risk that can be run. Will Rogers described credit risk best as involving not the return on investment but the return of your investment. As a rule, we tend to avoid any debt instrument with less than an "A" rating. We'll discuss credit ratings on bonds in detail in Chapter 7.

As bonds mature, the continual adding of new maturity rungs to a ladder of maturities can keep this process going indefinitely. Laddering a portfolio of bonds is another way to smooth out the ups and downs of interest rate changes.

What's a Bond Ladder?

A bond ladder, or laddered bond portfolio, is a series of bonds that each have a maturity date later than the bond prior in the succession. Think of a laddered bond portfolio as the investor's version of a vertical wine tasting.

We will examine the act of investing for income in greater detail in Chapter 7. Even if you do not yet rely upon your portfolio to provide you with an income, the chapter is still worth a visit. Suffice it to say that a representative fixed-income component should be a mandatory prerequisite in each and every portfolio.

CONCENTRATION: A CLOSER LOOK AT EGGS AND BASKETS

The collapse of Houston-based energy trader Enron was, to say the least, tragic for all of its stakeholders, both direct and indirect. Arguably, the greatest harm was suffered by scores of Enron employees who, in addition to losing their jobs, watched helplessly as their retirement savings, which had been pumped full of their employer's stock, came crashing down. We're not referring here to those senior executives under indictment for the criminal actions and inactions that led to Enron's demise; we're referring to the rank-and-file workers who continued to invest in good faith at the urging of their employer, in the process concentrating their retirement savings accounts to an ever greater degree in the shares of one company: in this case, Enron. For many Enron employees the collapse of their company meant a permanent shift in their standard of living to something far less desirable than what they had worked and saved for.

The lesson in the Enron catastrophe is that a portfolio can become dominated by one stock or market sector. This is a situation that often occurs in the portfolios of long-serving employees at major corporations. Most publicly-listed corporations offer employee share ownership programs and/or structure their compensation program to include an equity component. Over time, this can be deservedly rewarding. And, as a result, it is not at all unusual for a disproportionately large portion of an employee's net worth to become represented by the shares of their employer firm, a development that can also appear entirely logical. After all, if one of the cardinal rules of investing is to *know what you own*, then does it not make sense to have your largest holding in the shares of the company you likely know better than any other? Within reason, yes, but not excessively, and most definitely not to the point where the portfolio structured to help finance your retirement future is put at unnecessary risk.

KNOW WHERE TO DRAW THE LINE

All too suddenly the employee-shareholders of Enron, Nortel Networks, WorldCom and other fallen giants came to rue their extremely painful over-ownership of their company's stock. While employees usually fare well in their employee share ownership experience, these employee-shareholders unwittingly became part of spectacular, life-altering disasters. It is a lesson that is applicable not just to those who own shares in the companies for whom they work, but for anyone who has excessive exposure to any one stock or market segment.

Although we've already stated that a cardinal rule in investing is to know what you own, clearly this can easily be taken to extremes when it comes to employee share ownership. Stop to think for a moment how many times you have watched in amazement as another apparently invincible corporate bellwether is brought to its knees by changing technology, economic hardship or even scandal. Though tragic for shareholders, the problem is magnified many times over when your largest investment is also your place of employment and primary source of income.

A disciplined approach here is essential. Stop to consider the degree to which your employer's stock occupies your total net worth. You will need to have a discussion with your advisor (even if you are your own advisor) about the magnitude of employee share ownership that is appropriate for you. The investment policy statements outlined in Chapter 13 can help to clearly map out what the limits should be, but are useful only if you are determined to stick to your own guidelines.

A LITTLE OFF THE TOP, PLEASE . . .

Harm from portfolio concentration can manifest itself in other ways. If the company in question is part of a cyclical business (natural resources, consumer discretionary products, etc.) and as such the company's shares are subject to a high degree of price volatility, you'll need to be prepared for major fluctuations in the value of your nest egg. To mitigate volatility, you'll need to occasionally trim back the size of your position by regularly stopping to take profits on the way up. This will serve two purposes. The first is that it will force a discipline of not allowing any single position (or sector) to become an overwhelmingly large aspect of your portfolio. The second is that you'll be faithfully adhering to that old investment adage: You'll never go broke taking a profit.

The prudent investor must set limits on just how much of his or her portfolio should be dedicated to any one security or sector of the economy, regardless of how promising it may seem. This speaks to the issues of asset allocation strategies and investment policy statements, which we will explore in greater detail in later chapters. Again, it boils down to knowing where to draw the line so that the risks to you and your retirement investments are contained.

PACK RAT SYNDROME

Proper diversification may be a cardinal rule of successful investing, but just as there can be too much of a good thing (concentrated positions) there can also be too many inconsequential holdings. Time and again we see portfolios that have far too many holdings for their own good. They may not necessarily be poor investments, but invariably they are too small to have any meaningful impact on the overall portfolio, regardless of how well they do.

DR. SHARPE'S PRESCRIPTION

Michael subscribes to the view of the distinguished Dr. William Sharpe that there shouldn't be more than 15 to 20 different stocks or equity holdings in a portfolio at any given time. Why? Because beyond this number the benefits of diversification tail off steeply. Accordingly, Michael's initial advice on many portfolios he is shown is to begin the restorative process by weeding out superfluous holdings, ideally to no more than Dr. Sharpe's prescription. In the process, you'll also find that what's left becomes much more coherent and manageable.

CUT THE CLUTTER

Suppose a portfolio should be balanced 60:40 in favour of equities. Divide 60% by 15 and this gives 4% of the total portfolio value as the optimum size of each individual equity holding. If 12 rather than 15 equity holdings are judged to be the optimum, then the 4% becomes 5%. Individual holdings of this magnitude are meaningful. If they perform well, their overall impact will be positive; if one or two perform sensationally, the impact could be dramatic—and all portfolios should aspire to a grand-slam home run or two. If, however, a position begins to turn sour, the security in question will be much easier to spot if it is not lost amid the clutter of a portfolio that is excessively dispersed.

PLIGHT OF THE MUTUAL FUND INVESTOR

Mutual fund investors have a unique plight. It is not uncommon for this breed of investor to suffer simultaneously from both the Pack Rat Syndrome and portfolio concentration. Until the elimination of the foreign content rule in the 2005 Canadian federal budget, this had been an all-too-frequent occurrence among RRSP accounts. Under the terms of the foreign content rule, an investor could invest no more than 30% of the book value of his or her RRSP (or RRIF) beyond

Canada's borders. This rule invariably led many investors to stack, one upon another, a series of Canadian-based mutual funds. Each fund was presumed to approach the market from a slightly different angle, with the ultimate objective of additional diversification.

There is merit to this theory of style diversification, at least in principle. There are times when the growth method of security selection is the superior style. Similarly, there are occasions when value investing is significantly more rewarding. Where the theory can run head-first into practice is in a relatively small market, such as Canada's. The net result for investors can often be an unnecessary redundancy of holdings. Without knowing it, mutual fund investors can have concentrated positions in a handful of stocks and/or market sectors because their mutual fund managers all picked stocks from the comparatively limited menu that is the Toronto Stock Exchange. With the elimination of the foreign content rule, mutual fund managers will begin to choose stocks from the much wider global market in addition to that here at home, and this problem should ultimately sort itself out over time.

There remains, however, the central issue of a given mutual fund's mandate. Though a Canadian fund may invest some of its assets outside Canada, the bulk of its investments will be here. If you have an assortment of Canadian mutual funds in your portfolio, take a look at each of the fund's largest positions to smoke out redundancies. If you hold four Canadian equity funds, each of which list some combination of the big five Canadian banks among their largest holdings, chances are you've got a concentration issue. This is all the more so if, in addition to the mutual funds, you hold a bank stock or two (not a rare occurrence).

Be a Weight Watcher

Keeping asset weightings in line is a good way of maintaining necessary portfolio discipline and of controlling portfolio risk. It often includes a need to limit portfolios to an optimum number of holdings. This can mean adding to exceptionally promising holdings that are proportionately too small, taking them up to the desirable maximum weighting. Always remember there should be no more than an optimum number of equities in most individual investor portfolios. Each such holding must be meaningful in size. Excess holdings need to be weeded out to bring the portfolio to the optimum range of holdings (we prefer 15 to 20). This act alone will bring greater clarity to the portfolio, making it easier to spot and remedy problems much sooner than would ordinarily be the case with a cluttered portfolio.

This is not a prescription to give up on mutual funds. In fact, far from it. We're simply pointing out that many Canadian mutual fund investors are not getting the degree of portfolio diversification that they assume they are receiving. This is not the fault of the fund manager. It comes down to sloppy fund selection, which can be easily remedied by looking deeper within a fund family's stable of offerings and choosing funds with the same degree of care as you would individual stocks.

MAYBE KENNY ROGERS WAS RIGHT—*YOU'VE GOT TO KNOW WHEN TO HOLD 'EM . . .*

There was a dark period in Bryan's youth when his mother developed an affection (an unhealthy one in his opinion) for the music of Kenny Rogers, specifically, the album *The Gambler.* Day after day, the living room console stereo would reverberate with Kenny's dulcet tones belting out the title song's chorus—which has stayed with Bryan like an unsightly birthmark.

This Kenny Rogers classic lyric—of knowing when to hold on or fold— illustrates one of the most important and most often overlooked disciplines for successful investing: the sell discipline. All too often we are inundated with suggestions of what should be added to portfolios. Rare is the day when someone rings a little bell and says, "Okay, time to sell International Goose Grappler Inc." There's an old investment adage that says your first loss is your best loss. In his popular book on the fine art of investing, *How to Make Money in Stocks*, William O'Neil expands on the thinking behind the old first-loss chestnut, and recommends investors learn to take losses quickly and profits slowly. In real life, however, many investors do just the opposite, with unfortunate consequences.

Letting your losses run is often the most costly mistake an investor can make. You simply have to accept the fact that mistakes and unforeseen circumstances will make their way into your portfolio from time to time, despite your best efforts. This is something that is difficult, if not impossible, to control. However, what is under your control is your response to recognizing these mistakes.

One of the best methods of stripping away the emotion from the decision to sell a security is to put in place what is known as a stop-loss point, a predetermined price that triggers the sale of the given stock. This approach has the added advantage that if the security is on a downward trajectory and management is taking concrete steps to correct the related deficiency, you'll then be able to re-examine the company with cool detachment because you cut your losses earlier and are now faced with the question of whether to reinvest at a more attractive price. By then you might well have moved on to an even better, more lucrative investment opportunity and have a doubly nice choice to make, thanks to the discipline of stop-loss selling that automatically triggers action. We will explore in Chapter 8 how sell decisions are much better made this way than doing nothing or procrastinating endlessly.

A Humbling Experience

Forget your ego, offload your pride and never forget that investing is a humbling experience even at the best of times. You just can't fight the market. The market is not always rational. None of us can afford to fall in love with a company that is losing us money. Remember the words of William O'Neil, even if you have to swallow hard in the process: "Take your losses quickly, your profits slowly."

FALLING KNIVES

Yet another time-tested investment adage states that one should never try to catch a falling knife. That's good advice in the physical as well as the abstract sense, and is even more valuable today against a backdrop of seemingly unending corporate misdemeanours.

Catching a falling knife in the investment context concerns the act of picking up shares of companies that have dropped precipitously, usually after some catastrophic event. Sometimes, the rewards can be very lucrative. Not all that long ago, the shares of the once-mighty Nortel Networks, which had peaked at the $120 range, were trading at less than a dollar a share. For those who had the nerve to pick them up at that level, the recovery over the next several months was nail-biting, but highly profitable. The unfortunate reality for most is that they did not buy Nortel at $1. Even seasoned veterans fell victim to Nortel's siren song, purchasing shares of the company at prices considerably higher than $1, such as $60, $70 or $80, with the reasoning that "all of the bad news *must* be out by now!"

Unfortunately, investors who bought technology stocks early in the bear market after most NASDAQ-listed names had dropped by more than 60% from their peak levels have had a long wait just to get back to break-even. Many are still waiting as of this writing.

Michael likes to put a bit of a twist on the falling knives theory by preferring to pick up *fallen* knives, not falling ones. Using this rationale, investors know that they are not likely to grab on to a stock at its absolute lowest point. Instead, investors who shop among the fallen knives are more likely to buy shares of a company once recovery has already begun. Sure, they will forgo some potential profit, but this class of investor views the forgone profit as a small price to pay for the security of the higher probability that they own shares of a fallen rather than falling knife.

Admittedly, the temptation to grab hold of shares of erstwhile high flyers who have come upon hard times is understandably powerful. Consider the shares of insurance brokerage giant Marsh & McLennan, which in late-2004 dropped by more than 40% in just over a week following allegations of kickbacks and bid-rigging by New York State Attorney General Eliot Spitzer. A breathtaking plunge like this is just the kind of activity that ordinarily gets the contrarian investor's attention. (A contrarian is an investor who makes a point of going against the crowd.) In fact, many professional "vulture" funds make a living out of buying and trading in the shares of companies in deep distress. However, given the complexities and sheer number of corporate scandals to have emerged since the start of the new millennium, the successful catching of falling knives has become more difficult and dangerous than ever.

Don't Try This at Home

Knife catching is tough and often best left to professionals rather than casual investors. Bad news is often followed by even more bad news. Knife catchers with full sets of fingers are those who have moved in on a company after all bad news has been disseminated and when relatively good news is starting to emerge. The trouble is that the window of opportunity is exceedingly small and most knife catchers have been nicked more than once by moving too soon in anticipation of a turnaround.

Some corporate restructurings do work, making knife-catching on occasion a worthwhile endeavour. Witness Air Canada and Saskatchewan Wheat Pool, the former successfully brought out of court-protection from creditors while the latter toughed it out on its own. In each case the price was a steep dilution of their common shares to a point of worthlessness. On the other hand, court-protected companies like Stelco have been helped along by a sharp recovery in world steel markets, such that this falling knife could have been caught very successfully—but even then not without significant risk.

Buying fallen stocks when nobody else wants them can give the savvy investor who has done his or her homework a head start on the crowd. Nevertheless, being a contrarian investor isn't easy for the vast majority of individual investors. If you do like to dabble and prefer the stock markets to lotteries or the horses, and occasionally fancy yourself to be a catcher of knives, by all means set up a separate trading account, but always do so with a specific limit as to how much you can afford to lose. Never try to catch a falling knife in an RRSP or RRIF account. Though gains in RRSP or RRIF accounts are sheltered from tax, the trade-off is that if the trade turns into a painful loss, you will not be able to write off the resulting capital loss against capital gains on other transactions. In a genuine long-term investment portfolio, "never catch a falling knife" is an old Wall Street saying that is best heeded.

OTHER PEOPLE'S MONEY

Businesses regularly expand their operations through the use of borrowed capital. So do countless individuals. For example, home ownership would not be even close to today's level were it not for the innovative mortgage financing structures that began being introduced shortly after the Second World War and that have allowed consumers, Americans in particular, to raise fresh cash for spending by repeatedly re-mortgaging their homes at ever-lower interest rates.

Borrowing money for investment purposes offers a similar ability to gain financial *leverage*. For example, a $100,000 investment made half on borrowed money that rises in value by 10% to $110,000 will provide a profit of 20% on your original capital once the investment is sold and the loan paid off. This is the magnifying capability of leveraging in action. Unfortunately, the same principle applies in reverse as well. Going in the opposite direction, were the same investment to fall in value by 10%, the loss to the investor is actually a much more substantial 20%. Ouch!

Often, a company that has been funding its growth strategy primarily, or perhaps even exclusively, through the use of borrowed capital is referred to as being highly leveraged. Similarly, the act of borrowing to invest is often referred to as the act of leveraging, which, when used prudently, can work like an anabolic steroid on your net worth, adding muscle mass to your portfolio more quickly than would otherwise be the case.

Like anabolic steroids, however, leveraging can have nasty, undesirable side effects, introducing additional volatility to portfolios. The most common of these side effects occurs when a highly leveraged investor fails to meet a margin call and watches his or her equity disappear without the ability to recoup it. A margin call is a "send more money" call from your broker. One that is triggered by a drop in the value of your portfolio so that the account is in a status that is known as under margin. Please refer to the section entitled Margin Trading for more detail on the subject of investing on margin.

Financial Flesh-Eating Disease

When it goes awry, leveraging is more like the financial equivalent of flesh-eating disease, magnifying and accelerating the damage to your financial well-being. It's for this reason that leveraging needs to be handled with great care. The lesson? Using borrowed money to invest can dramatically magnify gains. Unfortunately, it works in the same manner in the opposite direction, magnifying losses and multiplying the degree of risk in an investment strategy.

You're likely familiar with the concept of leverage if you have ever:

- borrowed money to make a contribution to your RRSP
- bought securities on margin from your broker
- used a line of credit or term loan to raise money for investment purposes

Leverage can be applied to RRSPs, margin buying, short selling and mutual fund purchases; in other words, the uses are very wide.

RRSP LOANS

Early each year, the nation's financial institutions usually heavily promote RRSP loans in a bid to capture (for them at least) something akin to a two-for-one special. Short on cash after the holidays, and staring into the gaping maw of a potentially big tax bill? Fantastic! Your bank would love nothing more than to lend you the money to make an RRSP investment with them. This is all well and good, provided you don't over-borrow and you resolve that this kind of investment loan should be paid off quickly, even if your bank is offering it at their prime rate. The reason: interest charged on such loans is not tax deductible and can all too readily become an unwelcome millstone.

MARGIN TRADING

In a similar vein, brokerage houses offer margin accounts, which enable their clients to borrow money from the firm against the equity in their portfolio for the purpose of making additional investments. This "loan" works much like a secured line of credit, in that clients are charged interest on the outstanding balances and are free to repay the loan balances in whole or in part without penalty at any time. As long as clients have sufficient equity in their accounts, they are able to re-borrow and repay over and over again. However, under securities law, a brokerage house can only loan you a set percentage of the total value of your investment, and if the value of the outstanding debt exceeds the maximum permissible loan amount, the broker is then forced to make the dreaded margin call. That's the unpleasant conversation when you are asked to send more money in order to get back on side the percentage loaned, otherwise your brokerage will be compelled to sell some or all of the investment, even at a loss, in order to make up the shortfall. It is precisely for this reason that margin buying needs to be handled with utmost care.

In addition, being excessively leveraged through margin can rob you of control to effectively decide when certain of the securities held in your portfolio should be added to, trimmed or sold. This position of vulnerability is simple to avoid by making certain that you have plenty of excess capital available before engaging in buying securities on margin.

Dr. Graham's Prescription

One old-fashioned rule that stays in Michael's mind is to borrow for margin buying no more than the previous year's gain in the overall portfolio. Whatever approach you and your advisor decide upon, always set and keep to the strictest of limits on borrowing for investment purposes. Never forget that while borrowed capital magnifies gains, it also magnifies losses.

SHORT SELLING

The act of borrowing, from your brokerage, shares of a company you do not already own in order to immediately sell these shares is called short selling. This is another means of leverage that requires you to tread warily and is definitely not for the faint-hearted. For short selling to be a profitable venture, the shares of the company must drop in value so that you can buy them back on the market at a lower price, repay your broker and pocket the difference. The obvious risk to selling something you don't own is that the shares of the stock in question may rise rather than fall. The implication of this is that eventually you will have to pay back the shares to the brokerage from whom you borrowed. If the stock has increased in value, it will cost you more—sometimes considerably more—to buy the stock for repayment purposes. In the upside-down world of shorting, you make money only if the stock being shorted falls in value.

Margin requirements for short selling are generally much more stringent than for more conventional borrowing, and this can make short selling even more expensive.

MUTUAL FUND LEVERAGE

During the extended bull market of the 1980s and 1990s, banks got in on the lending act in a big way by providing term loans for investors wishing to invest in mutual funds. Clients were urged to make monthly payments that consisted almost entirely of interest on the loan, the line of reasoning being that steady appreciation in the value of the invested assets would render repayment of the loan principal unnecessary until such time as it could be repaid out of profits.

Investors, lenders and financial planners all benefited. Investors became enamoured with this type of financial planning strategy because it permitted them to effectively "rent" money, leverage their income and earn a profit on the rented capital. Similarly, the banks' security increased as the value of the portfolio increased. Borrowers paying interest only made these investment loans (sometimes referred to as leverage loans) highly profitable. Financial planners also loved the strategy because it enabled them to earn a commission on a large lump-sum investment all at once rather than the comparatively microscopic commissions they would make on investors' monthly contributions to their investment accounts. It was a situation in which all three stakeholders remained happy as long as the market continued its steady ascent.

Just as using borrowed money to invest has the positive attribute of magnifying gains, this form of investment can also magnify losses. The added tragedy is that losing money that is not your own doesn't alleviate the responsibility of having to pay back the principal and accumulated interest. In the case of brokerage firms, margin accounts with depleted asset values result in the "send more money" margin call, the worst kind of call a stockbroker can ever be asked to make to a client.

We are not fundamentally opposed to borrowing for investment purposes. Countries do it (the international benchmark limit being 60% of gross domestic product) and companies do it, so why not investors? It's no doubt that there are occasions when gaining this kind of leverage can assist materially in building lasting wealth, but always keep the prescribed limits in mind.

- Borrow no more for investment purposes than you are prepared to lose.
- Always remember that borrowing to invest is a strategy that is not for everyone.
- Respect the potential destructiveness of leverage.
- Avoid being seduced by the allure of tremendously magnified profits.

CONSIDER THE SOURCE

The hot tip. The inside edge. The smart money. In a world of supposedly efficient markets, the universal dream of investors is to find and act on information that is not widely available. Unfortunately, this perennial search can be carried to extremes in the hope that some obscure kernel of truth will provide an edge to score big gains in the market.

This isn't to say that great ideas shouldn't come from unconventional sources. Widely regarded as one of the savviest money managers ever to prowl the corridors of Boston-based mutual fund giant Fidelity Investments, Peter Lynch contended that individual investors can find good investment ideas by merely looking in the shopping cart when doing their weekly grocery shopping. (As well, this is corroboration of the teaching of Michael's former professor that "housewives make the best economists of all.") Lynch has always been a proponent of good old-fashioned common sense. The father of modern securities analysis, Benjamin Graham (sadly, no relation to Michael), believed similarly that sound investment should be based first and foremost on correct facts. This approach clearly rules out buying investments on a hunch or on a tip, or because an acclaimed guru is recommending it—as with Michael's purchase of IBM, to be related in the next chapter, a notable, but nailbiting, exception.

Make sure you do your homework before investing. Michael's research training has taught him to look critically at the record of the authors of research reports. He also always makes a point of reviewing the track record of the management of companies whose shares are being recommended. Genuine turnarounds are worth their weight in gold, but are very much the exception rather than the norm. It's much better to invest in a company with a reliable track record. Because it's your long-term retirement future that is at stake, you must have confidence in the source. For more information on research, please see Chapter 10, The Unfair Advantage.

TRIAGE: GET ON WITH THE HEALING

The injured being brought to a hospital's emergency department often have ailments requiring lengthy diagnosis and treatment. Just as often, however, on-the-spot action can be taken to stop the bleeding before deciding on remedial treatment and an ultimate cure. The same is true of ailing portfolios in need of proper long-term treatment, while self-inflicted wounds that can be dealt with then and there should be. Equally apparent are portfolios that are in obvious trouble because of a hodge-podge of shortcomings despite their owner's best intentions.

For an investment professional, just as hard as making obligatory margin calls is having to look well-meaning investors in the eye and tell them that their portfolios just haven't got it—that they can't possibly bridge that ultimate retirement gap because of an accumulation of self-inflicted deficiencies. This is a state of affairs that could also have come about as a result of a too-frequent chopping and changing of investment advisors and/or of a legacy of too many ill-suited, over-priced and illiquid investment schemes that looked better on paper than in execution. Even then, it is always better to face up to reality and begin the rehabilitative process as soon as possible. It's amazing how many investors immediately begin feeling better, despite the pain, the losses and the lost investment time needing to be made up.

In addition to a myriad of self-inflicted wounds, there's often an even bigger obstacle called "you" that needs to be dealt with in completing that all-important initial diagnosis. This obstacle requires separate recognition and dealing with, as we will discuss in chapters 3 and 4 of *Portfolio First Aid*. Never forget, however, that the ultimate diagnosis depends on you and your personalized investment goals down that long but exciting and satisfyingly-rewarding investment road.

Get treatment for your portfolio's various wounds quickly. As with many of life's endeavours, procrastination is often ultimately more costly than imagined. The sooner you embark upon the healing process, the sooner your portfolio will begin to gain momentum that will compound over the years. Over time, your now vibrant portfolio will make all the difference in the achievement of your ultimate goals.

CHAPTER 3

Tactical Errors
Mind Over Matter

To complete our diagnosis we need to look squarely in the eye of the investor's biggest potential obstacle of all: our own human failings. To err is human, but it's amazing nonetheless how we can get in our own way on the road to successful investing.

Like navigating a ship through uncharted waters, the essence of successful investing lies in the myriad of decisions that need to be made on your long-term journey. Most of these decisions will come in the regular portfolio reviews and accompanying adjustments that should be at the heart of every successful investment strategy. Others will need to be made in response to the unexpected, a subject we examined in detail in Chapter 1 and can promise plenty more of in the future.

Even the procrastinator, who ends up like the proverbial deer frozen in the headlights, will still have made a choice. Unfortunately, that kind of decision-making comes at the price of portfolios with weakened potential. Whether active or passive, large or small, these necessary *en passant* decisions will all add up over time to put their imprint on your portfolio and its ultimate degree of success.

FACTS AND REASONING
Benjamin Graham, introduced in Chapter 2 as the individual regarded by many as the father of modern-day investing, maintained that you will be proven right

if your facts and reasoning are correct. Following from this belief must be the making of sound investment-related decisions, and the taking of necessary portfolio action, in a world where change now takes place faster than ever before. You can be handed any number of "hot tips," or read a stack of books like this one to learn all you need to know about investing, but if your decision-making is flawed, whether because of incorrect information or failure to act, your portfolio will be as well.

Far too often, we are lulled into believing that someone has the so-called "silver bullet" that will deliver outstanding portfolio performance from here to eternity. Your authors have seen a lot of investment fads come and go over the decades, and have often wished someone did have all the answers. Life would then be so much simpler, predictable and more profitable—but also more boring.

EMOTIONS IN MOTION

The fact is that managing a portfolio in good times and bad is more a matter of process than of event. Along the way, you'll be asked to make hard and fast decisions. This is where the human element enters the picture, and must be faced and acted upon, rather than avoided. Even so, it's a risk that is all too often easier to recognize than to overcome.

For most investors, it is almost impossible to strip away emotion from the decision-making process. After all, this is money that has likely been worked for very hard and at considerable personal sacrifice. There can also be strong emotional ties to portfolios resulting from an inheritance. However, the inescapable truth is that our emotions must be brought under control if our minds are to remain clear enough to make the sound and timely investment decisions that will be called for.

Every 12-step program begins with the premise that before healing and recovery can take place there first must be the admission of a problem. Investors often have no trouble recognizing that a problem exists; for example, when swallowing hard at the bottom-line number on their portfolio statements. That sinking feeling can quickly take away any lingering subjectivity and inexorably bring them face to face with the need for something to be done about slumping portfolio performance.

It follows, therefore, that recognition of the emotions that cloud judgment and an understanding of how they can manifest themselves in the decision-making process become critical in achieving portfolio goals—and ultimate investment success.

Most if not all of us are psychologically hard-wired to think we are better off than we actually are. It's an ongoing self-deception that inevitably leads to decision-making errors. The tendency to become overconfident can also mean previous decisions being viewed as sound even when the evidence is to the contrary.

A century ago, Charles Dow, the founder of modern Dow theory and the man for whom the world's most famous stock market index is named, pointed out that the two most powerful human emotions investors can repeatedly expect to bump up against are fear and greed—polar opposites that can have a tendency to drive just about every investment decision and are all too often the root cause of clouded judgment. There are others, too. Highlighted below are these commonplace investor "sins" in what we see as the most logical sequence:

GREED

The 18th century South Sea Bubble fiasco and tulip bulb mania are both searing examples of how infectious greed can overwhelm even the most sensible investor. However, these and other examples of the herd mania that sweeps through the markets with regular monotony pale beside a speculative bubble that history will surely recall as the biggest—and also the most painful—of all time: the tech stock boom of the late-1990s.

We've mentioned Nortel Networks before, the Bell Canada spin-off that landed in the portfolios of thousands of rank-and-file Canadians. The timing of this "bonus" couldn't have seemed more fortuitous as technology stocks rocketed up and up and up, in Nortel's case to a peak of more than $120 per share. What a way to begin a new millennium! New-found riches danced before countless eyes. However, that was before the tech bubble burst and a grossly and, as it turned out, falsely inflated Nortel became a pricked balloon that subsided all the way to the $1 per share level. Few Canadian investors emerged from the Nortel experience unscathed. What a painful lesson for a great many veterans and neophytes alike!

In his book *Investment Blunders of the Rich and Famous*, Washington State University finance professor Dr. John Nofsinger addresses the common psychological condition in which people tend to believe they are better off than they actually are. To maintain this ongoing self-deception we tend to filter information to fit preconceived beliefs. Invariably, this leads to overconfidence and a psychological bias that can be devastating, as witnessed by investors in Nortel and a host of other high-tech stocks when the great tech bubble burst, as it inevitably had to.

In a similar vein, consider the popularity of lotteries, to many the very personification of greed. Statistically, lottery players have a better chance of getting hit by lightning than of winning the jackpot; yet, when these odds are raised, they will often give a glib response along the lines of "Somebody's got to win, and it might as well be me!" There is nothing wrong with this attitude, provided one is talking about a couple of dollars played at the corner store on a Saturday morning. However, it's a different matter altogether when applied to retirement savings that have taken a lifetime to amass. That's when the danger signals should really start to fly.

Often, the investment industry, in marketing its services to the public, panders to the same emotional biases used by lotteries in their advertising. Is it just a coincidence that many lottery and investment industry advertisements feature luxurious yachts, exotic villas, picturesque golf courses, etc.? The not-so-subtly implied message is "You *can* have it all, if only you turn your dreams over to us."

To be fair, the best investment firms are staffed with gifted professionals who spend their waking hours thinking about how they can better their competitively measured performances and, in the process, the investment performance of their firm's clients. We are happy to record many, many occasions when we've been witness to the kind of lifestyle enhancement that sound investing can bring about. Regrettably, we've also seen the lifestyle destruction that can occur when the investment dream turns into a nightmare. Almost without exception, that nightmare was spawned by greed, one of the most difficult of all human emotions to control.

PRIDE AND OVERCONFIDENCE

Similarly, the necessary decision to remove a losing holding from a portfolio is often deferred for no other reason than that making such a change would imply that a previous decision was a poor one. We mentioned previously that in his book *How to Make Money in Stocks*, William O'Neil, the founder of the widely read and respected *Investor's Business Daily*, advises readers to take losses quickly and profits slowly. Many of the investment decisions we are most proud of were rooted in that simple philosophy.

Regrettably, the instinctive response by the vast majority of investors is to do just the opposite. Pride can often drive investors to sell winning positions early to lock up a gain. This is logical enough, and is personified in that old saying "No one ever went broke taking a profit." The euphoric sense of victory that accompanies having made a good security selection can blind investors to the fact that a good investment is still doing its job within the portfolio. By all means trim successful holdings that become disproportionately large, but as a general rule, it's best to stay with winners and dispose of losers.

ENVY: KEEPING UP WITH THE (DOW) JONESES

The propensity to fall victim to the demon of greed, and its close relative envy, is greater than ever during times of surging market prosperity. This is the time when friends and co-workers begin bragging about the grand slam home run they hit from an obscure IPO (initial public offering). Greed is then being sparked by the entirely natural human response of envy. It's not unusual for that little voice in your head to pipe up and say, "If they can do it, I must be able to as well; after all I'm *much* smarter than they are…"

Running a portfolio free of psychological and emotional biases is comparable in many respects to playing golf. The most successful golfers will tell you that your only true competition is yourself. Trying to beat the other members of your foursome can be entertaining for a round or two, but if you're serious about reducing your handicap, you'll have to block out your competitive instincts to outplay those around you and focus, instead, on bettering your own game with every stroke. For investors, there is a similar need to recognize that envy can lead to contemplating levels of risk they might not otherwise have taken on or fully appreciated.

During the tech stock boom, even the great Warren Buffett began taking heat from his shareholders. With the bellwether NASDAQ Composite Index soaring into the stratosphere, and relative investment novices slipping headfirst into great fortunes in what seemed to be the blink of an eye, an increasing number of Berkshire Hathaway shareholders began urging their hero to "get with the times" and include at least a few technology names in the stable of companies held by Berkshire. Instead, the "sage of Omaha" held his ground, flatly rejecting the idea of investing in companies he didn't understand. If he and his worldly-wise partner Charlie Munger could not grasp the workings of a company and how it made profits for its shareholders, how could they presume to evaluate the worth of that company and its attendant investment risks?

Buffett not only had to withstand the ire of his own shareholders, but also the disdain of the North American investment media. A veritable cottage industry of print and broadcast journalists began discussing whether he had lost his Midas touch. In one humorous exchange with an exasperated questioner, Buffett was asked when he was going to retire. The answer, quick as a flash, was "Three years after I die." In the end, Buffett was vindicated by his rigid discipline of investing only in what he can understand. When the tech boom turned to bust, Berkshire Hathaway shareholders held on to their hard-earned dollars, while countless other investors fell by the wayside, many never to return.

Chart Your Own Course

Sadly, the majority of individual investors don't have someone as steadfast as Warren Buffett to guard against the envy that can often blur the otherwise sound judgment of even the most astute investor. This is why having a personal target rate of return for your portfolio is so critically important. We'll return to the vital question of "what's your number?" in more detail in Chapter 12. For now, however, we note its importance in determining what's wrong presently and in connecting this with the mapping of individualized portfolio strategies that will follow a proper diagnosis and in aiming to achieve longer-term, wealth-accumulation goals.

FEAR

Benjamin Graham also used to contend that "Investing is most intelligent when it is most business-like." These words, taken from Graham's epic work *The Intelligent Investor*, are *the* nine most important words in all of investing according to Warren Buffett, who developed them further to state that "Successful investing doesn't require extraordinary intelligence, but rather extraordinary discipline." Easier said than done, because at the opposite end of the emotional spectrum from greed sits fear. A healthy dose of fear can at times keep us from making foolish and costly mistakes. However, just as often, *irrational* fear can paralyze investors and foil decision-making in their best long-term interests.

How many times have we heard the cop-out, "I'd prefer to delay investing because…" The box that follows dates back to our beginning year of 1982 and drives home what dithering like this could have come to mean.

Dithering Diminishes Dollars

Waiting for the "right" time can be costly. There is always some crisis of confidence that successful investors must see beyond to make rational, informed decisions.

1982	Recession, pessimism rampant	1047*
1983	Stock market recovery premature	1258
1984	Record deficits, rising interest rates	1211
1985	Slowing economic growth	1546
1986	Stock markets ahead of themselves	1895
1987	Black Monday, October 19th collapse	1938
1988	Recession fears	2168
1989	Stock and junk bond market collapse	2753
1990	Gulf War	2633
1991	Recession, bear market	3168
1992	New U.S. political regime	3301
1993	Too many uncertainties	3754
1994	Rising interest rates	3834
1995	Stock markets ahead of themselves	5117
1996	Inflation fears	6448
1997	"Irrational exuberance" warning	7908
1998	Russian default, Long-Term Capital collapse	9181
1999	Y2K risks	11,497
2000	Bursting of tech bubble	10,786
2001	9/11, terrorism threat	10,021
2002	Severe bear market	8341
2003	Shattered trust (Enron, WorldCom, etc.)	10,453
2004	Iraq, contentious U.S. election	10,783

*The figures in this column represent closing levels of the Dow Jones Industrial Average at the end of the years shown.

When it comes to investing, there will always be reasons for backing off and procrastinating if you are so inclined. To move from the ordinary to the extraordinary, we've got to overcome the emotional biases. The most powerful of these is fear, which usually makes its presence known at precisely the point in time when valuations become their most compelling. The birth of the great 18-year bull market in the summer of 1982 and, most recently, the last gasps of the bear market in the autumn of 2002 are but a pair of examples. Just as greed can tempt investors to embrace already soaring securities, so fear can engender the procrastination that results in missing out on advantageous buying opportunities.

The chart overleaf illustrates how drastically investment returns would have fallen away had investors been out of the markets in what turned out to be the top 10, 20, 30 and 40 best trading days in the 1980s and 1990s.

Remember, you would have known what the best-performing trading days were only after they happened. In addition, each of these decades began with recession and a bear market, and each was to experience a major stock market collapse. Yet, they worked out sensationally well, with overall U.S. market returns averaging in the area of 17% in the 1980s and 20% in the 1990s. However, you would have shared in this prosperity only if you had stayed invested through thick and thin, using logic and reasoning, and guided by a well-structured investment plan (more on this in Chapter 13) within which to make strategic decisions along the way.

CREATIVE DESTRUCTION

Every so often a bewildered and none-too-pleased investor comes to see us with a portfolio that reeks of failure. The bewilderment often stems from the fact that at one point in their hapless portfolio's past it was a thing of beauty dancing along with, or perhaps even ahead of, the markets in terms of relative performance. By the time these investors get to us, though, the love has gone because the portfolio is stagnating or, worse still, has been bleeding cash for long enough to warrant a complete overhaul.

It is at times like these that we are reminded of the famous Harvard University economist Joseph Schumpeter and his writings on capitalism's capacity for "creative destruction." Though Schumpeter was referring to capitalism's unique ability to tear down and re-create itself based on the immutable laws of supply and demand, there is something very definite to be said for taking this principle into consideration in the management of portfolios.

Why It Pays To Be In The Market
– % Total Returns on S&P 500 – 1980's & 1990's

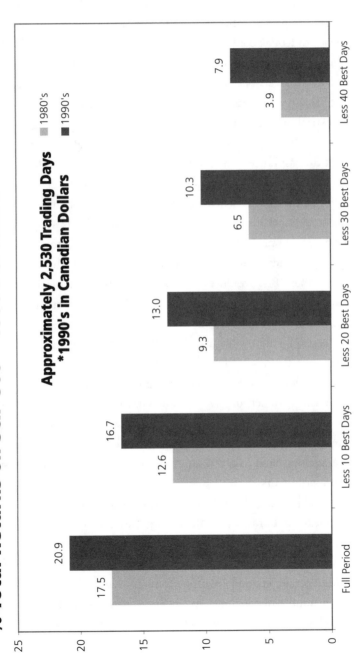

Approximately 2,530 Trading Days
*1990's in Canadian Dollars

Legend:
- 1980's
- 1990's

	Full Period	Less 10 Best Days	Less 20 Best Days	Less 30 Best Days	Less 40 Best Days
1980's	17.5	12.6	9.3	6.5	3.9
1990's	20.9	16.7	13.0	10.3	7.9

Sources: Bernstein Research, CI Global Advisors US

Steady, long-term investment performance can be achieved only by coping with continuous change. It's the same with companies that accept and adapt to a constantly changing world tending to outperform their peers and enjoying a much longer lifespan than those that cling rigidly to what has worked in the past. The example of Kodak couldn't be more revealing. Not long ago, Kodak was king of the photographic world. Then along came digital, which Kodak resisted at its own peril to discover, perhaps too late, that its world had changed, seemingly overnight. Today, what was once a proud component of the world-famous Dow Jones Industrial Average is in the process of radically reinventing itself to adapt to the new reality. In the process, it is playing an exceptionally painful game of catch-up without the assurance that it will be able to do so successfully.

By comparison, IBM eventually overcame a flawed decision to stick with its mainframe computers when desktop computers were taking over, but not before its stock market price was cut down by two-thirds and a change in top-level management was brought about by a board of directors with the courage to recognize the need for drastic action. There were many times when many doubted whether IBM would ever make the conversion successfully. *Who Says Elephants Can't Dance*, a book by IBM's legendary former chief executive officer Lou Gerstner, tells the remarkable story.

Michael can thankfully attest to how "Big Blue," which he had been prevailed upon to buy by a famous MIT professor at what turned out to be the sunset of the mainframe era, worked out very well for him in the end. Rather than taking the loss, he kept his patience and averaged down. In other words he purchased more shares at lower prices because he liked what he saw happening. Nevertheless, it took many years for that MIT professor to be proven right, for Michael to get back to his average cost, and for IBM to go on to become one of his most successful long-term investments.

Examples like these illustrate how creative destruction must also be part of the investment lexicon. For too long, the phrase "buy and hold" has been twisted from its original meaning to become code for a style of laissez-faire (i.e., hands-off) asset management that can often have little relevance in a pervasively changing world where strategies and investment tools that make sense today could be outdated in double-quick time. To illustrate what we mean, just think back to how technology-driven investments that were once representative of the tsunami-like force of change, and were believed necessary for growth in the 21st century, quickly became emblematic of devastating losses and fanciful pipedreams when a savage bear market set in to start the new millennium.

At the same time, embracing the concept of creative destruction need not be as radical or as revolutionary as one might think. For one thing, taking it to heart as an investor means much more than tearing down perceived conventional wisdom. Instead, creative destruction should be looked on as acknowledgement that in a global economy where constant change has become the norm, there is also a burning need to remain current on issues that could shape portfolios, as well as on tools to better manage portfolios. Exchange traded funds are a good example. There was a time, not all that long ago, when an investor who objected to the costs and direction of actively-managed mutual funds had few alternatives. The emergence of exchange traded funds dramatically altered the investment landscape for those whose preference runs to passive asset management.

It's not enough to have the information at your fingertips. You've got to be prepared to act when the facts tell you that you're in danger of being blown off course. Think of those poor misguided souls who in the early 1980s bought gold as it approached $800 an ounce, convinced that the yellow metal was well on its way to $1,000 and beyond. There wasn't a whole lot creative about gold's spectacular fall from its all-time high, but there sure was a lot of destruction to be found. Shumpeter's vision of creative destruction is just the kind of destruction you want, the kind where you are firmly in the driver's seat.

FORTITUDE

Think back to the first chapter in this book, and the birth of the great 18-year bull market in the rock-bottom summer of 1982. Statistics showed that the tide of individual investor capital began flowing into securities of varying descriptions only once the sustainability of the market's advance had been established beyond a shadow of a doubt, a process that took several years. There was nothing wrong with this, except that the most lucrative investment gains were missed by those who waited for the herd to dictate the direction of their portfolios, rather than by using their own logic and reasoning, and by having the fortitude (one of Sir John Templeton's favourite words) to back their judgment.

THE SEARCH FOR SPOCK

This brings us to the heart of the matter. The downfall of most individual investors involves a decision-making process that is too often coloured by emotion. For most of us, the dollars that reside in our portfolios represent considerable sacrifice and strain over a period of years, if not decades. When we stop to think of the effort that went into these life savings and the lifestyle hopes and dreams that they represent, we would need the emotional detachment of *Star Trek's* Mr. Spock to remain cool and detached about day-to-day decisions affecting our portfolio's well-being. Yet it's for this very reason that we need to each have our very own Mr. Spock to warn us away from speculative excesses, and to encourage us to see beyond unfounded fears in order to make investment decisions that are rational, not emotional.

Your personal Mr. Spock could be a trusted investment advisor, spouse, business partner or even a sibling. Regardless, that person should be someone with a sufficient degree of emotional detachment and expertise to have won your trust. You must then act on their counsel regardless of how hard it might be to swallow, or how painful it might seem at the time.

INVESTOR, KNOW THYSELF!

In the final diagnosis, you know you best. *You* are the owner of the portfolio that is being built and nurtured for *your* own distinct, long-term needs. Take stock of these needs, your ability to commit the time to study the information all around you, and your true comfort level with risk. Ultimately, the success or failure of your portfolio will come down to you. Regardless of whether you are a do-it-yourself investor or choose to work with a professional, you will need to be in tune with your own emotions and needs in order to make the required investment decisions that are most effective. Never forget it's always about *you*.

PART TWO

PRESCRIPTIONS

CHAPTER 4

You Need Professional Help!

In 1962, when Michael joined Wood Gundy as part of that fine firm's original research department, investors who needed professional help certainly didn't have much to choose from. Having been in operation for more than half a century by the time Michael arrived, Wood Gundy was only beginning to shed its image as a bond house to expand its offerings to include (gasp!) stocks. Mutual funds were fringe players, and the entire Canadian mutual fund industry was just a fraction of the giant it has grown to become today. Financial planning was available almost exclusively to the most sophisticated, well-heeled clientele. The friendly neighbourhood bank manager lent money, and could help you to make a little money with one of his bank's certificates of deposit, but was not the one you would turn to for advice on how to plan for your retirement. By comparison, today's range of choice of financial services and the types of professionals offering them is so broad it can be bewildering.

The Way We Were

"When I began my business career in 1962, Canada's financial services were built on four rickety pillars: an archaic banking system hamstrung by lending rate ceilings and other statutory impediments; venerable trust companies providing old-fashioned (even then) fiduciary and transfer services; old school investment dealers awakening to a life and world beyond bonds; and a fortress-like, mostly-mutualized life insurance industry steeped in tradition and actuarial dogma."

Michael Graham

"Money in the Bank"

The MoneyLetter: March 1999/First Report

Yet, in many ways the more things change, the more they stay the same. It's often been said that the two certainties of which we can still be sure are death and taxes. Change should be thrown into this cliché as well. Many changes can occur over the course of one's adult life: marriage, divorce, birth of a child, death of a parent or spouse, career opportunities, business ventures. The list is virtually inexhaustible, and we haven't even mentioned the inevitable ebb and flow of markets and economic conditions. Significant changes like these can end up directly or indirectly affecting the financial lives of most people and those who are dependent on them. The importance of investing to provide for our own *independent* financial futures in an environment of seismic change cannot be ignored and makes the need for professional help all the more imperative.

THRIVING ON CHAOS

In 1988, management guru Tom Peters published *Thriving on Chaos*, a book that at the time was considered to be a somewhat radical piece of business writing. In it, Peters prophesied a time when industrialized nations would be forced to defend their high-wage-earner status as Marshall McLuhan's vision of a global village became an increasing reality.

Peters anticipated the need for both blue-collar and white-collar workers to become more entrepreneurial in their approach to work, and for employers to foster an environment that not only encouraged but rewarded the free thinker who was able to quickly adapt to changing circumstances. As you are likely quite aware, that day has arrived.

Not only is change distorting the financial landscape beyond recognition (most often for the better, in our opinion), it is occurring at a speed never seen before. Once again, that diligent, trustworthy partner we stressed the need for at the conclusion of the previous chapter becomes a tremendous asset, and all the more so if he or she has access to timely, thoughtful research and analysis. In a world of constant and rapid change, you need someone to help you to adapt, step around unnecessary risk and seek out new-found opportunities to build (and safeguard) the value of your hard-earned dollars.

EVERYTHING OLD IS NEW AGAIN

To help investors cope with change (and sometimes to unwittingly exacerbate it), the financial industry is constantly dreaming up new financial instruments. Income trusts, REITs, hedge funds and fund-of-funds are all fairly recent additions to the financial landscape. The abundance of investment choices alone is a good reason to have a tried-and-true relationship with an advisor who has earned your trust—one who is keenly aware of your needs, wants, desires and fears.

Sometimes these new instruments are nothing more than a slick re-packaging of existing securities, the purple ketchup of the financial world designed more as a clever trap for fees than as a brilliant means of capturing greater gains for your portfolio. There are, however, just as many instances when a forward-thinking innovator does conjure something original that lives up to the accompanying marketing hype. In both circumstances, having a dependable partner by your side with the experience and expertise to separate the worthy from the unworthy among the plethora of candidates vying for your favour is a significant edge.

FINANCIAL ADVISORS: MORE FLAVOURS THAN BASKIN-ROBBINS

Depending upon where and how they are employed, the types of registrations held, their area of specialty and the infrastructure supporting them, some types of advisors will be more suitable to your own unique situation than others.

Generally speaking, advisors can be broken down into four categories:

1. financial planners
2. bankers
3. investment advisors
4. investment counsellors

Without a doubt there are highly competent, trustworthy professionals to be found in each category. Having an understanding of each type of advisor will help you to streamline the process of finding the most desirable match.

FINANCIAL PLANNERS

Financial planners take a holistic advisory approach that reaches beyond the composition and monitoring of client portfolios to deal with a wider range of financial issues including, but not limited to:

- detailed tax planning
- estate planning
- business succession planning
- asset allocation strategies

Financial planners are the one type of advisor to traverse all segments of the financial services industry. Their ranks can include stockbrokers who happen to offer complete financial planning services, and life insurance agents who have joined the fray in order to offer a more comprehensive array of services in an era where the life insurance policy is only one segment of an individual's finances.

The blurring of the lines among what were once distinct, if rudimentary, financial service pillars has not been lost on the nation's bankers, who now possess greatly expanded capabilities compared with as recently as a decade ago. Financial planning has transformed many job descriptions, but perhaps the most dramatically altered one is that of the bank loans officer (a title that was long ago tossed onto the ash heap of history). The banker who just set up your car loan would love nothing better than to look deep into your eyes and talk longingly about your retirement plans, all the while gently caressing a chart showing your projected assets in your golden years.

A Word of Caution

Be warned that there are very few restrictions on just who can hang out a shingle and call themselves a financial planner. Some are little more than salespersons. Before you entrust your hard-earned dollars to someone claiming to offer financial planning services, ask a few pointed questions. We'll offer some questions to ask later in this chapter.

Financial Planning Credentials

A certified financial planner is someone who has been granted the CFP designation by the Canadian Institute of Financial Planning. CFP holders have completed a rigorous course of study, and are required to complete a minimum number of continuing education credits each year in order to maintain their designation.

The Canadian Bankers Association (CBA) has established a parallel program for bank employees engaged in offering financial planning to the public. The CBA designation is known as the PFP, which stands for personal financial planner. Like

CFP designation holders, PFP designation holders are required to successfully complete a series of courses and keep up a regimen of continuous education.

Though reassuring, a designation like CFP or PFP is not necessarily a foolproof method of selecting a financial planner. We've been witness to some pretty egregious work performed by people holding designations that would suggest they should know better.

Fee-for-Service Planners

In Canada, most financial planners work on a commission basis, although there is also a small but hardy band of fee-only practitioners. Fee-only financial planners are financial planners who do not recommend specific securities or manage investment portfolios. Traditionally, fee-only planners tended to deal in more complicated financial situations. They have carried a reputation for being able to delve deeper in their analysis than those who offer financial planning as an added service to banking, insurance or securities offerings. The very notion of fee-based financial planning is, however, undergoing a significant transformation, just like every other facet of the financial services industry. Just like all of the other changes occurring throughout the industry, fee-based planners are responding to intensifying competition.

For many years, fee-based financial planners charged a fee for only preparing a detailed financial plan. No specific securities were to be sold to the client by this breed of planner. For those concerned about potential conflicts of interest, this was an ideal situation. The client of the fee-based planner would take the financial plan prepared on his or her behalf to a financial institution to execute the investment strategy contained within the plan.

More recently, the ranks of fee-based planners have increased quite dramatically, with a growing number of commission-compensated planners and advisors beginning to offer a fee-for-service component to their offerings. Later in this chapter we'll outline some of the questions that you should ask if you are shopping for a professional advisor, regardless of how they are compensated. The issue of fees versus commissions will be examined in detail in Chapter 11, Pay to Play.

BANKERS

In a bid to capture what is known in the industry as greater share of wallet, Canada's bankers have bent over backwards during the past two decades to shed their image as stodgy lenders of capital. In particular, the big banks have moved into what has come to be known as *wealth management* in a big way. Gone are the days of tellers waiting patiently at their wickets for you to come in with a deposit. Everyone in the bank is now an advisor of one magnitude or another. Don't let the bank's size and presumably good name sway how you view the value of their services. You've really got to judge the value of what is being offered on the basis of the person sitting across the desk from you. How? Ask for references. Find out how long they've been doing what they do. How often can you expect to receive progress reports on your portfolio?

There are many diligent, empathetic bankers/advisors. Over the years, both of your authors have developed lasting associations and friendships with bankers who have been of great service and value at one stage or another. Unfortunately, in our experience we have also been witness to many for whom it's just a job and to whom your life's savings represent little more than another file in their "in" basket. It's this latter group that must be quickly identified and avoided. Once again, asking the right questions at the start of the relationship will help you to better avoid potential disappointment later.

More often than not, any damage to your portfolio by your advisor will come not through acts of malice or commission, but rather through neglect and ignorance. Remember, it's a fast-paced, constantly changing world in which you really want to have someone who is "on their game" working for you. Unfortunately, and this is unique to the banking environment, banks seem to keep moving their best people around, promoting them to new responsibilities within the bank or to new locations. This type of advisor receives a large portion of their annual stipend in the form of salary, so if the bank tells them that starting tomorrow they are going to work at the branch across town, that's where they'll go. All of a sudden you'll find yourself with a new advisor, but don't assume you've been given the pick of the litter. Ask questions all over again. You're not being rude. Don't you think that same banker is going to ask you a lot of pointed personal questions if you want to borrow a little money? You're simply protecting what you've given a whole lot of blood, sweat and tears to attain. You simply must know who you are entrusting your money to. It's up to you to make sure you have an advisor who is going to do what it takes to help you build your investments and preserve the value of your portfolio.

Now let's say you've done all of your careful questioning and you've found a banker with whom you'd like to do business. Great! Please understand, however, that unless they're private bankers, who we'll come to later, these garden-variety bankers found at every bank branch across the country are trained to be generalists, not specialists.

The banker/advisor of today with whom you'd like to do business is someone who should be able to handle fairly basic, straightforward financial planning issues ranging from saving for retirement to developing a savings strategy for a child's post-secondary education financing. He or she should also be able to assist you with basic tax savings strategies, as well as rudimentary portfolio construction and asset allocation.

We use words such as "basic" and "rudimentary" because of the constraints placed upon the banker/advisor by both the terms of their licensing and the offerings available from their employer institution. Thus, the overwhelming majority of banker/advisors you are likely to run into are licensed to handle little more than mutual funds and term deposits. A small, albeit growing, number are moving to the next step, which is to be fully licensed to handle a wider range of securities, including stocks, bonds, exchange traded funds, income trusts and insurance-related vehicles, such as segregated funds. If you are just starting out, and your needs are not highly complex, dealing with an advisor who works primarily with mutual funds and term deposits is not necessarily a bad thing.

These folks are often required to wear more than one hat over the course of their average working day. Hence, their focus is not always going to be on the portfolios under their care. For this reason it can be a blessing in disguise that the banker/advisor sticks with mutual funds for equity-related investments, whereas a qualified third party (the fund manager) makes the day-to-day decisions over what stocks are to be bought, sold or held.

Private Bankers

Sitting at the high end of the advisory food chain offered by the chartered banks are private bankers. These are advisors specially trained and equipped to service more than just individuals. Private bankers are frequently called upon to work on complex financial situations involving high net worth families and closely held small to medium-sized businesses.

The scope of the services offered by private bankers is quite diverse, placing this category of advisors in a position to become intimately involved in the lives of their clients. At its most basic level, private banking permits the client to have a dedicated banker who can go to greater lengths than would ordinarily be the case to link personal and professional banking, as well as to coordinate investment, tax and estate planning with philanthropic goals.

It is not unusual for the clients of a private banker to have financial needs that transcend international borders. To meet these needs, private bankers also offer offshore services, such as offshore trusts that can sometimes be used as estate planning vehicles and to protect assets from litigation risk, as part of a tax planning strategy.

The services of a private banker are generally limited to a bank's wealthiest clients. Often, the minimum asset threshold is $1,000,000. The banks aim to offer highly sought-after clients like these one-stop shopping for all their financial needs. In some instances, this is ideally suited. It is not unusual, however, for a well-heeled investor to prefer an "unbundling" of services, and to opt to use a private banker for some services, a brokerage house for full service, a discount broker for some other services and an investment counsellor for other facets of his or her financial life.

INVESTMENT ADVISORS

Still known in the industry and by much of the general public as stockbrokers, or just simply brokers, investment advisors ply their trade at the nation's brokerage and investment firms. Traditionally, they did little more in the way of advising than counselling their clients on which stocks, bonds or mutual funds to buy or sell. However, over the last couple of decades, this pillar of the Canadian financial services industry has, like the others, undergone a significant transformation in a bid to offer a more holistic approach to meeting client needs.

The evolving nature of the services offered by investment advisors (and everyone else making a living in financial services) has been in response to intensifying competition and a bid for greater market share.

Customarily, most investment advisors have been compensated on the basis of commissions charged for securities bought and sold, although that too is undergoing a significant change. Growing numbers of clients and their advisors are moving from a commission structure to a flat fee, expressed as a percentage of assets under management as the preferred method of payment. Please refer to Chapter 11, Pay to Play, for more information on the relative merits of paying fees versus paying commissions for the work performed by your investment advisor and his or her firm.

Brokers, whether they operate under the title of Investment Advisor, Investment Executive, Financial Advisor or Financial Consultant, are, by the nature of their relationship with their employer firms, afforded considerable latitude in choosing the mix of products and services they may offer their clientele. Some tend to be the more stereotypical, transaction-oriented advisor, focusing their energies on making specific recommendations of securities, usually stocks and bonds, to be bought and sold. The better advisors long ago recognized the cold, hard reality that they cannot be all things to all people, and have more often than not tried to specialize in the aspects that play to their strengths, though this is not to say that an investment advisor who is adept at picking stocks is unable to select appropriate mutual funds or recommend an asset allocation strategy.

Variety Is the Spice of Life

Walk into any brokerage office across Canada and you will find as many different ways to manage your money as there are advisors in that office. With a few exceptions, most of the styles offered are quite valid on their own merits. This lack of uniformity is the polar opposite of the advisory experience found at the nation's bank and trust companies. The lack of uniformity is not, however, a structural flaw in the offerings of the brokerage. The greater choice can be quite liberating, depending on your needs and wants. Once again, the selection of an advisor requires great care and diligence. Ask your friends who they have as their advisor. This could be particularly important, since many established advisors do little or no advertising, gaining many of their clientele through referral from satisfied existing clients.

Uncomfortable talking to friends or family about your finances? Take some time to attend a workshop or seminar delivered by a brokerage office. You've probably already found that broker-sponsored and -conducted workshops are pretty easy to find, and are usually fairly close to home if you live in an urban setting.

The Entrepreneurial Edge

Often, investment advisors reach a point in their career paths where the sheer size of their clientele, together with growing competitive pressures, will compel them to take on staff and build teams of specialists to satisfy the needs of a growing and diverse clientele. It's not uncommon to find teams staffed with an administrative assistant, an associate advisor specializing in financial planning and an estate planning specialist. The members of the team are almost always paid for by the lead advisor rather than by the advisor's firm. This highlights a critical point of differentiation between brokers (or whatever else you want to call them) and those bankers/advisors who are employed by banks, trust companies and credit unions. The overwhelming majority of brokers in Canada are required to be listed as employees of their respective firms for tax and regulatory purposes. In reality, though, they are independent contractors, in that this class of advisor makes his or her living solely from the work performed for their clients.

That there is no salary for advisors to fall back on in tough times can serve as both a blessing and a curse for clients. On the positive side of the ledger, the broker or investment advisor, like any small business owner, lives and dies by their clientele, and as such is more likely to be keenly aware of their clients' needs and wants—their livelihood depends upon it. On the negative side is the potential for conflicts of interest, and excessive trading designed to boost commission revenue.

Caveat Emptor

There are many excellent advisors to be found among the nation's large and small brokerages. Just as we stated with regard to bankers, there are some investment advisors who are best avoided. How do you know when you're sitting with a champion for your money versus an accident waiting to happen?

Just as we stated earlier that a bank's size and reputation alone are not necessarily assurances of quality, the same can be said of investment houses. Brokerage firms are required by law to maintain compliance departments, which monitor the work of their advisors, keeping watch for unethical and illegal activity. Generally, though, this is less about quality control than about keeping the advisor's work in line with national and provincial regulations. Most, if not all, compliance departments are simply not designed to extend their oversight any further than that. The ultimate responsibility for ensuring that you are receiving the best of what your advisor has to offer rests on your shoulders. It is, after all, your money.

INVESTMENT COUNSELLORS

The standout characteristic of investment counsellors is that they are independent to the point where they have no business affiliations or gainful associations that could prejudice the arm's-length decisions they make on behalf of their clients.

As Michael can testify after 36 years as an investment dealer and seven (and still counting) as an investment counsellor, the focus of an investment counsellor's business is to advise individual clients and, in most instances, to manage client portfolios on a discretionary, fee-paying basis.

Discretionary vs. Non-Discretionary

The overwhelming majority of the investment counsellors in Canada manage client accounts in their care in what is known as a discretionary manner. This means that the counsellor, after having their client sign an agreement, makes buying and selling decisions on individual securities on behalf of the client without seeking approval for each trade. This contrasts with a non-discretionary relationship which is more typically found with investment advisors and in which the client must approve each trade before it is placed.

Investment counsel firms range from single practitioners to large entities with many partners. For clients of these firms, the appeal, aside from an investment performance track record, is the ability to confer directly with the people making the day-to-day investment decisions. This permits the client to direct the investment counsellor toward or away from certain types of securities. This could be on the basis of closely held personal ethics or for reasons of religion. Though this degree of flexibility is also available with an investment advisor who is picking individual securities with his or her clients, it is not possible if the advisor is using third-party asset managers, such as mutual funds.

Investment counsellors also spend the largest proportion of their time, some even as high as 80%, on research for clients' portfolios. This is in marked contrast to others who spend the majority of their time interacting with clients. The investment counsellor model is designed for those who hire managers and monitor them, rather than instruct and direct them. The fact that so many investment counsellors have the Chartered Financial Analyst (CFA) designation only adds to the research depth and the "unfair" research advantage they can bring to their clients (refer to Chapter 10).

Investment counsellors can combine unbiased investment advice with the ongoing management of their clients' investment portfolios. For economy of management, investment counselling and management relationships typically work best with higher net worth investors, usually $1,000,000 and up.

THE GOOD, BAD AND UGLY: CHOOSING THE ADVISOR THAT'S RIGHT FOR YOU

Once you meet an advisor with whom you think you might like to work, there are some basic questions that need to be asked to help ensure you have a good professional and personal fit. Here are the seven questions that we believe should be at the core of an introductory meeting with a potential advisor.

1. How long have you been an advisor?
2. What are your average assets under management *per household*?
3. How many clients (households) do you serve?
4. What is your investment philosophy?
5. Who is on your support staff?
6. What can I expect from our relationship?
7. What are your credentials?

Now let's look at the seven questions in detail in order to help you to "smoke out" vitally important information at the introductory meeting, and ultimately make an informed decision on choosing the advisor that's right for you.

How Long Have You Been an Advisor?

Pretty self-explanatory here. Pick a number of years' worth of experience that you feel is adequate, and go from there.

What are Your Average Assets Under Management *Per Household*?

This is important because it will let you know where your family's total assets stack up against the advisor's other clients. Don't believe any altruistic platitude about treating everyone the same. That's one of the all-time great red herrings, ranking right up there with "No, that dress does not make you look fat at all."

Size Matters

Let's not kid ourselves. The simple truth is that larger clients get more time and attention than small accounts. When you work on commission (or fee for service) for a living, it really is a dog-eat-dog world. Ideally, what you want from your prospective advisor is some degree of selectivity. We're not advocating an elitist approach, though. An established advisor with a thriving practice eventually arrives at the point where they need to manage their workload intelligently. That means they've either got to set some criteria for becoming a client, or they've got to take on more help. If the prospective advisor states that they work only with clients who have $200,000 to invest, and you have $225,000, how much attention do you think you will garner? It would be nice to think that an advisor will treat all clients equally, and in some rare instances that is exactly what happens. Often though, while all clients are treated equally, some are more equal than others. It is preferable to be a big fish in a small pond rather than a small fish in a big pond. Take care to choose an advisor for whom you will not necessarily be their largest client, but you'll not want to be the smallest either.

How Many Clients (Households) Do You Serve?

Let's be practical here. Although Mr. and Mrs. Jones technically count as two separate clients, chances are they are sitting down with the advisor together and therefore they should count as one. What you're looking for here is an advisor with a healthy, stable clientele.

In the late 1990s, Merrill Lynch conducted a study in which it found that the optimum number of households an advisor could properly service was 175. Since that time, technology has advanced to a point where we believe the number could be safely moved up to 250. If your prospective advisor responds to your question with a number that is considerably higher than this, ask the advisor if there are any associate advisors on his or her team. Many of the most experienced advisors have one or two (sometimes more) associates on staff to help shoulder the workload. If this is the case, the 250 figure can be raised even higher based on the size of the advisor's staff.

Chances are that an advisor with a small clutch of marginal clients is not going to be around for very long. The exception to the rule is if you are looking at someone still early in their career. More seasoned clients may not want to deal with a relatively inexperienced advisor, regardless of their gold-plated academic credentials (more on that in a moment). However, a young client with fairly straightforward needs can often do quite well with a rookie broker, growing with that advisor over a span of many years as they both grow older together and move forward professionally. The risk, of course, is that the rookie becomes one of the many unfortunate "washouts" who don't last long enough to celebrate many anniversaries with the firm. Should this come to pass, your protection lies in the firm that your now-former advisor was employed with. Investment firms have a fiduciary responsibility to you, their client, and as such are obligated to make certain that another qualified individual is in place regardless of whether or not your advisor left the business of his or her own volition.

If your firm assigns your account to another advisor, your responsibility is to take the time to get to know this advisor and to satisfy yourself that this person is right for you. If it's not a good fit, there's nothing wrong with saying so. In fact, it's preferable if you speak up early, calling the branch manager and asking to be reassigned to someone more suitable for you, rather than suffer through a poor relationship. That time spent brooding could wind up being quite costly to you. Once again, it's your money. If you don't speak up in its defence, who will?

What Is Your Investment Philosophy?

With this question, you are trying to ascertain exactly what it is that guides the advisor sitting before you in recommending one type of security over another. Many people are a little too intimidated by their lack of investment acumen to ask this basic question, or back off when the advisor starts to speak in jargon. Don't be—you needn't be Alan Greenspan. If the advisor lapses into some Gregorian chant, spewing acronyms and financial linguistics, stop them dead in their tracks. Ask for clarification. You are not stupid, and more likely than not the advisor is not trying to baffle you with some bullish balderdash. You simply want to ensure that you are both speaking the same language.

Many professionals who work in a technical field have the annoying tendency to slip into their professional mother tongue. Think of your doctor, your auto mechanic or, worst of all, the 17-year-old kid who just fixed your computer. If the advisor and his or her intentions are honourable, when pressed for clarification the advisor should be able to explain his or her investment philosophy in terms that anyone can follow. If the advisor is unable to explain his or her motives in a language you can understand, move on. Good communication is essential to establishing trust, and if he or she is either unable or unwilling to communicate something as fundamental as investment philosophy, you're going to have problems sooner than later.

The advisor you are interviewing may state that he or she uses third-party managers such as mutual fund managers to look after the portfolios in his or her care. Another might state he or she has a value bias, for example favouring the security selection method pioneered by Columbia University finance professor Benjamin Graham and made famous by Warren Buffett. The point of the exercise is not to become an expert on investment styles, but rather to learn whether the prospective advisor is working from a core set of principles that guide recommendations. A serious professional will be.

Who Is on Your Support Staff?

Even the most determined workaholic advisor will inevitably get sick, go on vacation, attend a conference, etc. Who's minding the "shop" while the advisor is away? Who can you call if you need help? How long has that help been with the advisor? What are their qualifications?

Good advisors, like any competent professional, invest back into their practice. That means going beyond the very basic level of administrative support offered by the major firms, and hiring (and paying out of their earnings) additional staff such as associate advisors, estate planning specialists and financial planners. They don't need to have all of these people on staff, but a growing advisory practice is labour intensive, and adequate help ensures that the client experience remains very personal.

What Can I Expect from Our Relationship?

The courting stage is a good time to establish up front what each of you expects from the relationship being considered. Set the parameters of exactly how often you and the advisor are going to sit down and review your money's progress. Will all meetings be face to face? Perhaps some will be done over the phone. How often can you expect statements? Can you take a peek at your accounts via the Web? Is the advisor going to call you with a recommendation and expect an answer on the spot? You should see some evidence of a process that the advisor works through in all client relationships. This process should be flexible enough for some degree of customization, yet not so flexible that the advisor loses focus and spends most of the day scrambling from one emergency to the next.

What are Your Credentials?

Given a choice between a relatively inexperienced advisor who has gold-plated academic credentials and a seasoned veteran, a veritable graduate of the fabled school of hard knocks, we lean toward the latter. This is not to say that we are dismissive of higher education. If you should happen upon someone with the scrappy instincts of a street fighter *and* the refinement of a rigorous formal education, you may have found just the right combination to work for you.

"Persistence and determination are," as a famous Calvin Coolidge quote states, "omnipotent." Successful investing is something that is as much an art as it is a science. The instincts and sound judgment that are a necessity for a qualified advisor can be acquired only with the patina of time. The world of investing is not a neat and tidy place. People lie, circumstances change and rules are written and rewritten. Through it all, the desirable advisor continues to evaluate, study and contemplate the most suitable path for his or her clients, sifting all available information through the filter of experience.

Credentials, such as a CA, MBA, CFA or, heaven help us, a PhD, are valuable to say the least. At the same time, as Michael can attest, they are only a complement to experience—not a substitute. Formal education prior to the start of an advisor's career provides an excellent foundation on which to build. As noted previously, we live in a world of constant change in which continuous study is a vital ingredient to success. This includes formal as well as informal study. The formal study is generally found in the continuing education requirements that licensing bodies now place upon advisors. In the course of meeting these obligations, many advisors will acquire professional designations such as the CIM (Canadian Investment Manager), CFP (certified financial planner), CFA (Chartered Financial Analyst) or FCSI (Fellow of the Canadian Securities Institute), all of which are offered by qualified professional organizations. These designations (and others) are a good sign that your advisor is committed to maintaining sharp skills and a well-stocked arsenal of knowledge.

Still, your authors have met some advisors who, despite outstanding academic and professional qualifications, fail to stay abreast daily of changes that can adversely affect the client assets in their care. Keeping up can be as simple as reading the newspaper daily, and can extend as far as membership in professional organizations where an exchange of ideas is possible. Ask your prospective advisor where he or she gets the best investment ideas and how he or she stays on top of developing trends. The answers will reveal a great deal about the level of persistence and determination residing deep in the advisor's belly.

GET HELP

Our bias on this matter is undeniable. Yes, we earn our living from providing advice to investors on just exactly what they should be doing with their money. We are, arguably, in a good position to speak to the importance of having proactive, professional and ongoing counsel on the management of your nest egg from someone you know and trust. Change, as we noted in the opening paragraphs of this chapter, is constant, and occurring more rapidly than ever before. We have seen countless examples over the years of investors who have been caught "offside" with their investments when circumstances have changed quickly, or when investment decisions have been made with dated information.

We do live in the information age, and while we may be more informed than ever, the sheer volume of available information can easily lead to clutter and ultimately confusion. This is where a dedicated professional, one whose interests are inextricably linked to your own, can cut through that clutter, keep you abreast of shifting circumstances and put you in a position to make more informed investment decisions.

It's Always About You

Working With an Advisor

The title of this chapter could be mistaken for an accusation hurled during a marital spat. Our context is much less contentious. We like to think of the client/advisor relationship as being a little more comparable to the kind of close-knit, trusting relationship that you might have with your family doctor (minus the request to turn your head to the right and cough). The common denominator in both kinds of relationships is the focal point: you.

In the last chapter, we underscored what we believe to be a very strong case for having some kind of professional advisor by your side to assist you in making intelligent investment decisions on a consistent basis. Here we continue the line of reasoning to describe the working parts and responsibilities inherent in a successful working relationship with any type of advisor.

A PROCESS—NOT AN EVENT

There exists a widely held misconception that declares successful investing to be composed of a series of unconnected, random events. The hot tip, the discovery of the savvy fund manager and the high-concept investment all come to mind. The truth of the matter is that successful investing is really much more of a process than an event or even a series of events.

THE STARTING POINT: FINANCIAL TRIAGE

The first step both of us take when consulting with a "wounded" investor is to embark upon a process to uncover the investor's wants, needs and risk tolerance. Most advisors, to varying degrees, employ these same basics of the financial planning process in work with their clients.

At its core, financial planning is a six-step process, and is evolutionary by nature. Simply put, the process should be flexible to adapt to changes in your financial circumstances. The six-step process we subscribe to can be summarized as follows:

1. **Fact finding:** The first step in the process is for you and your advisor to have a very frank conversation about your current financial situation. The more information that you can bring to this meeting, the more value you'll receive in return. The advisor will look at your financial life from several different vantage points, and will need to have an up-to-date snapshot of your investments.

   Before this advisor can perform an effective analysis of these investments, though, it is important that they place the information in the proper context. It is for this reason that you should let the advisor know the details of your debt obligations, your income and your income source(s). The discussion of the source of your income is important because the advisor will want to determine whether there is much of a risk of an interruption to your cash flow. If so, special attention will need to be paid to the issue of liquidity and an adequate emergency reserve.

   There are a growing number of advisors who have taken to using a detailed questionnaire to gather information. This is over and above the mandatory Know Your Client (KYC) form. Often this is quite useful for both you and the advisor. The questionnaire is usually sent out to the client in advance of the initial, fact-finding meeting, permitting you to take your time to complete the forms in detail. The questionnaire helps to ensure that important information is not overlooked during the initial meeting and can evolve into a wide-ranging dialogue.

   Though we are not opposed to the use of such questionnaires, we caution that the questionnaire itself is not to be used as a replacement for a fact-finding meeting itself. There needs to be that all-important human interaction. This is particularly true when it comes to the measurement of your tolerance for risk. Too often, attempts have been made to try and boil down an assessment of an investor's appetite for risk by putting forward a series of questions, each designed to "smoke out" the respondent's true attitudes toward risk. More often than not, this form of risk measurement offers little more than a means of "pigeon-holing" the investor to a specific, predetermined profile, and ends up doing more to save the advisor's firm from litigation than getting at the heart of the matter.

One of Bryan's clients is a retired psychometrist (someone who does psychological testing/evaluation). Her concern regarding the use of questionnaires to assess a client's attitudes toward risk and reward is that while they may represent a fairly accurate portrait of the investor's deep-seated beliefs, the responses can be tainted by recent successes or failures in the market. Bryan's client recommends, and we concur, that if a questionnaire is to be used at all, it should be revisited at regular intervals (semi-annually or annually) to ensure that the responses given during the initial meeting are still a valid reflection of the respondents' viewpoints. Use these questionnaires as the tool they were originally intended to be: an adjunct to a vigorous discussion on the issue at hand—*you*.

2. **Objectives:** Once your advisor has a firm grasp on where you stand today, the next logical step is to have a discussion about exactly what it is you wish to achieve. This can be a fairly wide-ranging conversation, and should encompass everything from your medium- to long-range financial aspirations to the "terms of engagement" with the advisor.

   Any investment/financial plan worth its salt should be guided by a rational set of objectives. Should your objectives prove to be unrealistic, it is the responsibility of the advisor to bring reality into focus. A good advisor will not tell you just what you *want* to hear. The truly professional advisor will tell you what you *need* to hear.

   As part of the objective-setting process, you and the advisor should establish some fairly basic ground rules over the degree of risk you are prepared to withstand. The advisor will talk through some hypothetical situations with you. Take, for example, that you purchase an investment for $50 per share and a month later it is worth $100 per share. How responsive will you be to an advisor's suggestion that you trim back a portion of this wildly profitable position? Going in the opposite direction, let's assume for a moment that you purchased income trust units at $19 each. A week later the Bank of Canada increases interest rates by 50 basis points and as a consequence, the units drop in price to $14. Assuming that nothing has changed with respect to the income trust itself, how willing would you be to permit your advisor to purchase more units for you at the new, substantially reduced price? For your own sake, it's a good idea to be brutally honest. There's no medal for bravery to be had. Too often, we've seen clients exercise ill-placed bravado only to learn too late that they are not the reincarnation of J.P. Morgan they had fantasized themselves to be. If you're going to make a mistake, it's a far better thing to err on the side of caution than hubris.

3. **Analysis:** It is at this point that you and the advisor may wish to go your separate ways for a few days while the advisor analyzes the information provided to him or her at the initial meeting. An assessment of your assets, liabilities and cash flow will allow the advisor to put your present financial state into a context with your objectives. This will permit your advisor to map out a strategy that is unique to your own needs. This strategy will likely but not necessarily include a tune-up of your investments, recommending the elimination of some in favour of others, corrections to errors of omission and the scaling back of positions that have become disproportionately large in relation (or too small so as to be meaningful) to all other securities in the portfolio.

4. **Asset allocation**: After completing a thorough analysis and its attendant recommendations, the advisor will be able to wrap the investment strategy around a comprehensive asset allocation strategy. We'll delve into the art and science of asset allocation in detail in the next chapter. For now, let's simply describe what asset allocation is, and set it within the context of the six-step process.

Asset allocation comes in two forms: *strategic* and *tactical*. Recognizing the risk and reward characteristics of the three main asset categories—stocks (equities), bonds (fixed income) and cash—strategic asset allocation seeks to strike an appropriate balance among the categories to meet at the intersection of a particular client's need for growth and tolerance for risk. Tactical asset allocation begins to take shape after the strategic asset allocation has been established. With tactical asset allocation, the primary goal is to spread the assets within the equity component among various market sectors or geographic regions in order to maximize investment performance while managing risk.

Strategic asset allocation tends to remain more rigidly fixed in place over an extended period of time, and is usually only dramatically altered if and when the client faces a significant change in their objectives brought on by a life-altering change such as retirement.

The objective in this stage of the process is to sketch out the broad parameters of the strategic asset allocation. Details as to when rebalancing should occur will be covered in the Investment Policy Statement, which we will focus on in Chapter 13, The Roadmap to Peace—and Prosperity.

5. **Security selection:** When the process is running smoothly, the effort expended in step four should flow seamlessly into step five. This is where tactical asset allocation enters the picture, and the detailed work of building an Investment Policy Statement begins. The advisor will draw upon his own analysis of your agreed-upon needs and overlay his understanding of asset class characteristics to narrow down the range of appropriate securities. From there, the advisor can lay out his recommendations for your approval.

6. **Maintenance:** Warren Buffett has been lionized as a monumentally patient investor, so much so in fact that he once famously answered the question "What is your ideal holding period?" with one word—forever. It would be a mistake (and a tragic one at that) to assume that buy-and-hold investors do not need to periodically make adjustments to their investment holdings in response to changing developments that can affect the values of their investments. Even Mr. Buffett has been known to do just this. Over time, some securities will grow more quickly than others. Though we are advocates of the theory of letting one's winners "run," on occasion it will be necessary to scale back positions that have become disproportionately large. This takes us back to asset allocation. A well-thought-out asset allocation strategy will recognize the need to make adjustments, and will set out guidelines for when and if rebalancing should occur.

THE FINANCIAL FULL MONTY: YOUR RESPONSIBILITIES AS THE CLIENT

The quality of the advice that you receive from your advisor will be determined in large measure by the quantity and quality of the information you provide to him or her. You really need to open up to this person, letting them know exactly what you hope to achieve. Of equal importance is the need to disclose your deepest, darkest financial fears.

Investors with significant financial holdings occasionally wish to have their assets spread among a handful of institutions and/or advisors. Depending on your situation, this often turns out to be a less-than-ideal situation for both you and the advisor. You simply need to provide full disclosure. The advisor must be able to see "the big picture," including assets that you may not yet be ready to bring under his or her responsibility. The primary advantage of this financial "full monty" is to permit the advisor to offer recommendations that are set within a proper context and to avoid redundancies and errors of omission.

Letting your prospective advisor in on your deepest fears allows the truly professional advisor to have a true understanding of your tolerance for risk, and your need (if any) for growth. Opening up completely alerts the advisor to any potential life-altering changes that could prompt a significant change in the investment strategy you have asked him or her to formulate for you. If you suspect, for example, that the company for which you work may be coming out with an early retirement package in six months, and you are a likely candidate, put that on the table. Even though the anticipated event may never come to pass, you will be far less prone to disappointment if the advisor with whom you have trusted your life savings has a contingency plan in place all the same. Remember: the more you give, the more you receive in terms of reliable advice.

WHAT'S IN IT FOR ME? RESPONSIBILITIES OF THE ADVISOR

As we discussed in the last chapter, the advisor has a responsibility to provide you with a clear understanding of his or her investment philosophy. He or she should also provide you with a plan for managing your portfolio and ultimately helping you to reach your goals. There should be no deviation from the plan unless the proposed changes are first discussed with and approved by you. Just as your communication with the advisor needs to be frank and complete, so too does the advisor's communication with you. The advisor needs to outline which services he or she will be bringing into the relationship personally, and which services will be contracted out.

The benchmark(s) against which your portfolio's performance will be measured should be set out in advance by the advisor and agreed upon by you. Most advisor/client relationships are non-discretionary. This means that the advisor makes adjustments to your investment holdings only after consultation with and approval from you. In order to make it easier for you to make well-informed investment decisions, your advisor will want to periodically provide you with an overview of the current market and general economic climate. Without having the relevant facts before you, how can anyone reasonably expect you to make sound investment decisions? A little client education will make both the advisor's job and yours significantly easier.

COMMUNICATION BREAKDOWN

To have the most productive, lasting relationship with any financial professional, it is imperative that expectations from the relationship (for both you and the advisor) are clearly articulated at the outset. One point that often leads to relationship-ending friction between client and advisor is the matter of personal contact. Of course, it is reasonable to expect that your advisor will proactively get in touch with you if and when circumstances demand your immediate attention. It's those occasionally lengthy periods where there is no pressing matter to attend to that problems creep in.

You need to ask yourself how often you want or need to meet with the advisor. Is it reasonable for you to expect a quarterly portfolio review? Perhaps, but be prepared for the possibility that the advisor, eager to retain your business, could make promises that he or she may not be able to keep. Ask how often the advisor thinks portfolio reviews should be conducted and negotiate, if necessary, from there to arrive at a frequency of contact that you can both live with. If you're considering working with a busy advisor who has a large clientele, there may be associate advisors with whom you can connect if your need for contact is greater than the amount of time the advisor ordinarily can spare. Having occasional portfolio reviews conducted by a competent associate and supervised by your advisor is preferable to inconsistent contact from a harried, distracted advisor. The emphasis here should be on the consistency and quality of reporting your portfolio's progress beyond the regular statement. This accountability should include proactive advice when necessary.

You and your advisor should also have a blunt conversation regarding your expectations for portfolio performance. An ethical, professional advisor will not permit you to set unrealistic expectations, nor will they prey upon the basic human instincts of fear and greed.

KEEP IT REAL

Avoid setting hard targets such as "I need a 10% return on my money every year." The markets are in a constant state of flux. You will be far less prone to disappointment if you set a range of returns in relation to previously agreed-upon market averages, or if you set a long-term rate of return. For more information on setting performance targets, please refer to Chapter 12, What's Your Number? Benchmarking Performance.

Just the Two of Us

Some of the principles that apply to a happy, long-lasting marriage can also apply to the functioning of a happy, long-lasting and mutually rewarding relationship with your financial advisor.

- Full disclosure: Let the advisor see all of the working parts of your financial life, but don't stop there. Speak openly about your hopes and fears.
- Demand feedback: Regularly scheduled progress reports serve several purposes. They keep the advisor accountable to you, reduce the chances of something important "falling through the cracks" and raise your level of awareness. This last point will, over time, make it easier for you to make well-informed investment decisions, resulting in fewer regrets.
- Set goals: How will you know you're winning if you don't keep score? Work with your advisor to set attainable goals that reflect your overall objectives.

IT'S A TWO-WAY STREET

Solid, enduring marriages are built on a foundation of good communication and trust; so too are long-standing, mutually rewarding relationships with financial advisors. Once the trust has been established and the communication flow agreed upon, respect is the next ingredient called for in this recipe for success. Respect needs to extend from both parties in the relationship. You, as the client, need to remain mindful of the fact that the professional with whom you are working is likely devoting most of their waking hours to their craft. The terms of their licence require the advisor to engage in many hours of ongoing study. Through the firm at which your advisor is employed, there is access to timely analysis of securities and market trends that most individual investors have neither the time nor inclination to source out on their own.

In a similar vein, it is imperative that the professional financial advisor demonstrate the utmost respect for you, their client. Regardless of the corporate name on their business card, it is the client for whom the advisor works. The advisor needs to remain mindful of what often has been many years of hard work and sacrifice that went into amassing the capital that is now being put before the advisor to care for. The best advisors carry an attitude that the client is doing the advisor a tremendous favour by bringing their business to him or her, not the other way around. The professional, conscientious advisor never loses sight of just whose money is at stake and what those dollars represent. The finest advisors always remember that it's always about you.

CHAPTER 6

Balancing Act
Asset Allocation Strategies

USING ASSET ALLOCATION TO MINIMIZE RISK AND MAXIMIZE RETURN

Winemakers will often blend specific quantities of various grape varietals to create a wine that has certain unique characteristics—something that is more than the sum of its parts. This is the essence of asset allocation. By putting together certain combinations of the three main asset classes of stocks, bonds and cash, an investor should be able to create a portfolio that is unique to his or her own tolerances and preferences for risk and reward. Like the wine that is the result of a careful blending of grapes, a portfolio successfully blending divergent securities should result in something much more valuable than the sum of its parts.

STAY SHARPE

William Sharpe is a professor emeritus at Stanford University who rose to international prominence with his Nobel Prize–winning work in 1990 on measuring investment risk and expected return. Sharpe's advice to a Toronto audience in 2002 was to be certain to "diversify, diversify, diversify." His accompanying view: "We're looking at a risky future, and the question is what price we are going to pay to hold stocks." The entire objective of asset allocation is to give the investor the greatest opportunity for gain with the smallest degree of risk, something Dr. Sharpe has spent much of his adult life studying.

There has long been a misconception, though, that getting the asset allocation right outweighs the importance of careful security selection. It's a misconception fuelled in part by studies that have shown asset allocation to be a critical determinant in portfolio performance. Though we agree that getting the right asset mix is highly important to a portfolio's long-term success, sloppy security selection is still going to hamper progress. However, get the two working in harmony and you will have a thing of beauty.

We'll cover the selection of both fixed-income and equity investments in the chapters to follow. For now, let's keep the focus on how these asset classes can work together for the common good.

STOP SWINGING FOR THE FENCES

To be an active investor is to be an optimist. Even though we've been investing for ourselves and for clients for many years, we still can't help getting excited at the opportunities each day brings. It's also human nature to want to knock the proverbial ball out of the investment ball park. Experience has taught us, however, that swinging for the fences every time results in little more than a whole lot of strikeouts. The more sensible strategy, to carry on the baseball metaphor a little longer, is to strive to get runners on base every time and to advance runners through consistency. A successful asset allocation strategy will help you to do just that. Ultimately, it's consistent returns that you should be seeking from your overall portfolio.

ZIGZAG

The three main asset classes behave differently at various points in time. Ideally, you want some portion of your portfolio to zig while others zag. By studying the historic patterns of various types of investments you will notice that the three main asset classes seldom move in a synchronized manner. Sometimes they even move in opposite directions. This is what is known as an inverse correlation, and is central to the risk-busting attributes of asset allocation theory. The net result of the entire exercise is to give you more consistent portfolio performance by having less dramatic peaks and troughs in value.

Study after study has shown that in periods of 10 years or more, equities provide the best total return on investment. Bonds, by comparison, offer stability and income-generating potential. Cash (and its equivalents) pay little, yet offer safety and are useful for meeting unexpected liquidity needs. Various combinations of these three distinct asset classes will deliver differing quantities of both risk and return. Finding the balance that meets your own unique requirements lies at the heart of asset allocation.

TAKE A LOOK IN THE MIRROR

You can't even begin to draft a comprehensive asset allocation strategy until you have given some serious thought to your objectives. Are you building wealth to support yourself in retirement? Or are you accumulating capital to pay for your children's post-secondary education? Once you have articulated your goals against considerations like these and put them into a time frame, a little soul-searching with regard to your risk tolerance will be in order.

Risk comes in many forms, which we will explore in Chapter 9, Running With Scissors. For now, we remain primarily concerned with the big picture, and as such are seeking something more like a blood pressure reading of portfolio volatility and your tolerance for it.

As mentioned in Chapter 5, a number of financial institutions have developed detailed questionnaires for the express purpose of gauging attitude toward risk. While we have no quarrel with the use of these questionnaires, we feel very strongly that there is no substitute for human interaction. Your responses to a questionnaire should be nothing more than the starting point to a deep conversation with your advisor on the subject at hand. This conversation about risk should be part of the fact-finding that we described in the last chapter.

Some factors that you and your advisor need to take into consideration before drawing up an asset allocation strategy for you include your:

- age (and that of your spouse, if applicable)
- career status (early, approaching retirement, already retired, etc.)
- sources of income
- financial resources, including your net worth
- current and anticipated financial obligations

Your objectives, tolerance for risk and your responses to the factors just listed will determine the direction that your asset allocation takes. Having someone push the dialogue along with thoughtful questions will help you and your advisor really get to the heart of the matter.

TACTICS AND STRATEGIES

Within the scope of asset allocation theory are two distinct methods of asset allocation: tactical asset allocation and strategic asset allocation.

Tactical asset allocation is an exercise in getting an appropriate balance among the three main asset classes of stocks, bonds and cash. The practitioner of tactical asset allocation's priority is to be in the right place at the right time to optimize the trade-off between risk and reward depending on prevailing market conditions.

Strategic asset allocation is all about striking a balance between risk and reward that meets the risk tolerance of the client. The investor utilizing strategic asset allocation use the historic risk and performance characteristics of the three main asset classes as the primary determinant over how much of the investor's portfolio should be directed to each respective category.

TACTICAL ASSET ALLOCATION

Tactical asset allocation strategies tend to focus more on maximizing the investor's rate of return than on managing risk, so by definition the investment time horizon here tends to be more short term than would otherwise be the case. Think of tactical asset allocation as taking more of a market timing approach to investing than its cousin, strategic asset allocation. As such, it has historically tended to be more suitable for trading-oriented investors or professionals. For many individual investors, tactical asset allocation is often best executed through a mutual fund, hedge fund or investment counsellor dedicated to the practice.

Tactical asset allocation strategies are notorious for their lack of breadth, yet we firmly believe they can be of great benefit to investors, particularly looking to the future. A growing number of investment industry leaders are expressing the belief that investment returns over the next decade will be much more modest than in the previous two. In this expectation, a significant debate has erupted over the relative merits of buy-and-hold investment strategies versus more proactive, opportunistic strategies. Those investors seeking to beat the major market averages may find particular appeal in tactical asset allocation strategies.

STRATEGIC ASSET ALLOCATION

Strategic asset allocation differs from its sibling tactical asset allocation by tending to be more focused on investor risk tolerance and long-range objectives. It also takes on more of a long-term perspective, usually five years or greater.

---

100 Minus Age

There are dozens of cookie-cutter-type asset allocation strategies that appear to be wonderful in theory, yet often are sadly lacking in practice. One such example is the "100 minus your age" strategy. With this strategy, the investor subtracts his or her present age from 100 to find out how much of his or her portfolio should be allocated to equities. Or, inversely, that present age should be the percentage allocated to bonds and fixed-income. The implied message here is that as investors age, their tolerance for risk subsides, and so also should their allocation to stocks.

This asset allocation strategy strikes us as one that raises more questions than answers. No consideration is given for changes in an investor's personal circumstances, such as sudden wealth. What happens if investors in question are a married couple with a significant age difference? The list goes on, but we won't belabour the point. In our view there is simply no substitute for a detailed conversation about your needs and wants with a qualified, experienced professional.

It's not unusual for an investor to employ both methods of asset allocation simultaneously, with tactical asset allocation as a component of a larger strategic asset allocation strategy.

THE EFFICIENT FRONTIER

First off, stop thinking about William Shatner! The efficient frontier has nothing whatsoever to do with *Star Trek*. What it does concern is a two-dimensional, historic analysis of how various mixes of asset classes have performed over extended periods of time.

Nobel Prize laureates Harry Markowitz and William Sharpe (yes, that guy again) took a scientific approach to examining how to build what they referred to as risk-efficient portfolios. They examined both the historic risk, as measured by standard deviation, and the historic return of a wide range of investments. They were then able to take this data and plot it on a graph to vividly illustrate how certain combinations of securities can often yield surprising results. Take, for example, their revelation that a portfolio composed 100% of U.S. Treasury bonds had a higher standard deviation (meaning it is subject to more price volatility, which many investors define as risk) than a portfolio split 40/60 between equities and fixed income. In addition, that 40/60 portfolio had a greater rate of return than the all-bond portfolio. Talk about revolutionary research!

Balancing Risk & Reward
– The Efficient Frontier

Source: Merrill Lynch

What the efficient frontier teaches us is that it is possible to arrange holdings in portfolios so as to strike an effective balance between risk and reward. It's interesting to note that the efficient frontier is a curved, not straight, line. Where do you belong in a curved-line scenario like this? All in stocks (and/or related equity products) and the risks could be too high; all in bonds (and fixed-income equivalents) and the investment returns could be too low. Nor is it a case of simply placing an *x* where you think you'd like your portfolio to be balanced. Your optimal point on the efficient frontier will depend on many considerations: your age, your resources, your financial and income needs now versus later, your tax bracket, your tolerance for risk, your sleep-at-night point—also the ultimate size your portfolio will need to reach to achieve what you want from your investments. Your position on the curve and the road map to get there are topics we will focus on in Chapter 12. Suffice to say at this point that correct portfolio balance is essential in both.

Yet, despite the best efforts of the investment industry's sharpest minds, asset allocation remains as much art as science. Capital markets are dynamic in nature. So too are investor wants and needs. It is for this reason that all of today's advanced technology hasn't been able to boil asset allocation down to an entirely mathematical formula. Hence, we encourage investors to put their asset allocation strategy down in writing, ideally as part of a comprehensive Investment Policy Statement.

For obvious reasons, we stop short of suggesting that asset allocation decisions be cast in stone. Your needs will change over time, as will your ability or desire to take on certain volumes of risk. It's clearly important that you and your advisor remain in regular communication. When clients inform us they intend to retire in two or three years, we can work with them at a thoughtful, pedestrian pace to adjust their portfolios to meet their changing circumstances. When they walk into our offices and declare that they are going to retire in two days' time, there is little room for subtlety and in the ensuing rush a significantly higher probability of an unfortunate oversight.

REBALANCING: LIPOSUCTION FOR YOUR PORTFOLIO

Over time, some segments of your portfolio will grow faster than others. The inevitable result is that its shape will begin changing in much the same way as a middle-aged guy with a tendency to overindulge in pizza and beer. Pizza guy will need months of cautious food intake, and grunting and sweating at the gym, to get back into shape. Mercifully, the health program for your portfolio needn't be as strenuous.

As we noted earlier, you'll need to set some parameters in your asset allocation strategy on how far you will be willing to let a segment grow. When a segment or security pushes past this predetermined threshold, you'll know it's time to trim back the position. This is in no way a repudiation of what we stated in Chapter 2, where we paraphrased *Investor's Business Daily* founder William O'Neil's dictum that you should always take your losses quickly and your profits slowly. Stopping from time to time to trim back overweight positions in your portfolio is a good discipline that helps to ward off the risk of something else we described in Chapter 2, Portfolio Concentration.

WHERE DO WE GO FROM HERE?

What should you do with the capital you've now taken from the fastest-growing segment(s) of your portfolio? The simple answer: Reinvest into the sector of the portfolio that is under-represented. This is exactly what happens more often than not. On occasion, however, it may be prudent to reserve judgment on where to reinvest. This may be due to unpredictable market conditions, when wise investors will set aside some of their profits in the cash section of their portfolios for use later when, presumably, prices may be more advantageous to the buyer.

STRIKING THE RIGHT BALANCE

The search for the balance between risk and reward that meets your needs continues from the objective-setting stage through to an examination of the trade-off between risk and reward. You should view these two attributes in tandem. Understanding the characteristics of major asset classes, and even specific securities, will go a long way toward unravelling the riddle of *your* asset allocation.

The reward part of the risk-reward pairing, stated otherwise as investment return, is already almost universally understood. Rates of return are regularly published for major market averages, mutual funds, stocks and so on. With most fixed-income investments, the yield is known right from the start, assuming of course that you are planning to hold, not trade, these securities. What is much harder to quantify is the risk side of the equation.

STANDARD DEVIATION

Standard deviation has, over time, grown to become the investment industry's preferred method for measuring risk. It's a calculation of volatility of the investment returns of a given security. The higher the standard deviation number, the riskier the security. Take as an example two very different mutual funds. One, a bond fund, will carry a standard deviation rating that is substantially lower than an emerging markets-based mutual fund. This is not to say that one is superior to the other. The standard deviation will be vastly different for each because one fund (the bond fund) has historically demonstrated much less pronounced fluctuations in value than has been the case with the emerging markets fund.

The popular view among the statisticians who generate standard deviation ratings is that a minimum three-year time horizon is necessary to effectively come up with a standard deviation rating for a security. Three years is considered a sufficiently long enough period of time to establish a trend for a given security, reducing the risk of the analysis being tainted by abnormal short-term fluctuations. By using standard deviation, investors can then make a more direct comparison between similarly mandated securities.

One criticism frequently levelled against standard deviation is that it tends to treat above- and below-average performers in exactly the same manner. It's fine and dandy to declare that your mutual fund carries a below-average standard deviation, but poor investment returns are still poor returns. Chances are, what you are most concerned about is the possibility of losing money. That's why we prefer to use other means of measuring risk and reward in addition to standard deviation.

PEAKS AND VALLEYS

An alternative to standard deviation is to take a look at an asset class or a security's best and worst 12-month periods. Arguably, this is a much more "back of the envelope" means of understanding risk and reward characteristics. Nevertheless, it remains useful in that it offers a sense of an asset class or security's potential tendency for extremes by looking at actual performance figures.

Taking the probability of capital loss into consideration, it becomes readily apparent that time *in* the market is as important, if not more important, than the timing of entry points. John Templeton used to make the case very convincingly, as illustrated in the accompanying chart. This is particularly true of equity investments, provided, of course, that a portfolio is sufficiently diversified and stocked with high-quality names.

The "Best" Time To Invest
Average Annual Rates of Return 1972-1996*

Investment Made at:

Market high each year	16.9%
Market low each year	18.0%
DIFFERENCE	1.1%

Conclusion:

> **The best time to invest is whenever you have the money.**

*Results of $5,000 invested each year for 25 years in the Templeton Growth Fund
Source: Templeton

We'll be the first to admit that the prospect of avoiding losses is not what gets investor pulses racing. Rather, it's the prospect of having the money you've worked so hard to attain working even harder for you. The simple fact that you need your money to grow in order to fund your objectives (remember those?) then leads to the question "How much is enough?" This is where a look back at historic returns can serve as a guide.

If you are looking for a high degree of growth over an extended period of time, following an asset allocation strategy focused primarily on capital preservation through the extensive use of bonds will lead to disappointment. Similarly, funding retirement income needs with portfolios composed almost entirely of growth-oriented equities is a recipe for disaster. The inescapable fact is that if you want superior growth, it will be necessary to take on incrementally greater degrees of risk in the composition of your portfolio. Similarly, if you are a risk-averse investor, and your portfolio is structured to reflect that preference, don't expect the kind of return on investment that would inspire a late-night infomercial. Alan Greenspan, the revered U.S. Federal Reserve Board chairman, perhaps summed it up best of all when he repeated an often-used colloquialism: "No one has yet invented the free lunch."

MUTUAL FUNDS AND ASSET ALLOCATION

It certainly would be nice if everything could be wrapped in a tidy package, kind of like the endings to most Hollywood movies. Unfortunately (or fortunately, depending on your point of view), life is seldom like a Hollywood movie. And this handy little bit of philosophy (which we offer to you at no extra charge) applies in equal measure to asset allocation.

Managed financial products, such as mutual funds, often have their own ready-made asset allocation. There is a wide assortment of mutual funds practising tactical asset allocation as part of their mandate. As well, virtually every fund company offers at least one balanced fund; that is, a fund that aims to strike a predetermined balance between fixed income and equities.

If you and your advisor are working on a detailed asset allocation strategy that includes, for example, a balanced fund in the mix, take a moment to crack the fund open to see how the assets are allocated. The best place to look for this information is in the governing prospectus, which will tell you what the constraints are and the maximum degree in any direction toward stocks, bonds or cash that the fund is permitted to move. Once you have this information, it becomes easier to see whether and how the fund will fit within your desired asset allocation.

INCOME TRUSTS AND ASSET ALLOCATION

Given the high yields offered by most income trusts (we include royalty trusts and real estate investment trusts [REITs] in this discussion, but for simplicity will refer to them all simply as trusts), it is not unusual for investors to include trusts in their asset allocation as part of the fixed-income segment. This is a mistake. Income trusts are high-yield equity investments. Though most are sensitive to interest-rate fluctuations, the vast majority of the income trusts trading on the market today are much more closely correlated to movements in the stock markets than the fixed-income markets. Remember, the primary objective for holding bonds is capital preservation, with income generation a favourable by-product, whereas income trusts are equity investments with an attached income stream that is not guaranteed.

INTERNATIONAL EXPOSURE AND ASSET ALLOCATION

For as long as many of today's generation of active investors can remember, the Canadian dollar has been the anaemic cousin to many of its international counterparts, especially the U.S. dollar. In 2003, however, the tables were turned when the mighty greenback began to fall from its very high perch as the world's pre-eminent currency. This, along with surging commodities markets, helped raise the value of the once-feeble Canadian dollar against a number of currencies—the U.S. dollar in particular.

Through the better part of 30 years, Canadian investors were taught that investing beyond Canada's capital markets was a sound means of adding additional portfolio diversification. As the Canadian dollar sank, foreign investments translated back into Canadian dollars received a currency-induced boost. Hence, adding global exposure often tended to increase a portfolio's performance while simultaneously reducing its risk profile.

With the rapid appreciation of the Canadian dollar by more than 30% against its U.S. counterpart between the spring of 2003 and the spring of 2005, the strategy of heavily emphasizing non-Canadian investments was turned on its head. Just as a portfolio would receive a currency-induced lift when international investments were converted back into depreciating Canadian dollars, those same international investments were dragging down portfolio performance when converted into rising Canadian dollars.

Although Canada is one of the world's largest countries geographically, it is relatively small from an economic perspective, representing a mere 3% of world GDP and capital markets. And while a number of world-class investment opportunities call Canada home, it is obvious that there is a much wider, almost limitless, selection beyond our borders. Furthermore, the 2005 Federal budget's elimination of foreign content restrictions on registered plans such as RRSPs and RRIFs will make it significantly easier for Canadians to invest more of their retirement savings abroad.

International investing makes perfect sense when the opportunity for growth exceeds the risk posed by currency exchange. We tend to steer away from global bonds as an asset class because there is simply not enough potential gain to overcome the risk posed by currency fluctuation unless you are an institutional investor with the capability and clout to bid for large quantities of bonds, negotiating a yield advantage. However, equity investment in other countries' companies or indexes is an altogether different story. If the growth potential offered by a non-domestic security is superior to what can be found closer to home, then you're on to something. If not, stay home: at least you won't have currency conversion risk issues to contend with.

THE PORTFOLIO FIRST AID CAFÉ MENU

Talk about mixed metaphors! The range of possibilities for blends of the three main asset classes is virtually limitless. What we offer you here is a tasting menu of basic asset allocation strategies that we have used successfully. Each of the strategies that follow are strategic (rather than tactical), and have been designed to meet the lifestyle needs many investors face at one time or another.

To keep things simple, we've focused these strategies on the Canadian markets, although they could easily be adjusted to suit an investor seeking global exposure. Forgive the tortured metaphor; we were very hungry when we wrote this chapter.

Capital Preservation Hall: *A hearty selection of bonds topped with a glaze of money market instruments. Seasoned with an accompaniment of hand-picked, conservative, yield-bearing equities.*

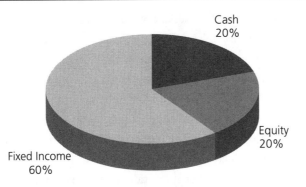

This asset allocation would be suitable for an investor who is highly risk-averse. The substantial cash component is there to offer stability and a high degree of liquidity. Given the minimal yield on cash (money market) securities, a 20% equity weighting offers a counterbalance that portends improved long-term returns. It should be assumed, however, that the kind of equities selected for this segment of this portfolio will lean toward the more conservative end of the spectrum, ideally toward equities that provide a dividend yield.

Though it may be natural to assume that this asset allocation strategy is designed with the stereotypical widows and orphans in mind, it could just as easily be utilized by someone facing a period of uncertainty; for example, a business owner struggling through the uncertain start-up phase of his or her enterprise. This person may need to lean on personal savings until the business gets on its feet. As such, the high level of liquidity and low level of capital risk offered by this capital preservation model makes for a very nice fit.

Jacob's Ladder: *A progression of strip bonds garnished with a broadly diversified equity mutual fund.*

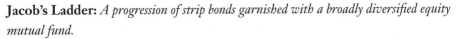

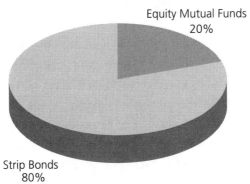

A variation on the capital preservation model is the mutual fund/strip bond ladder. This strategy works well for RRSP accounts where the investor is highly averse to the risk of losing capital. Its beauty is the recognition that a strip bond is a future sum of money purchased at a discount.

The 80% of the portfolio allocated to strip bonds in this example is invested in a series of strip bonds known as a ladder. Upon maturity they will add up to the value of the original investment in the entire portfolio. As such, even if the equity component is entirely wiped out, the matured value of the bonds will protect the original capital. To ensure that this strategy remains risk-free, stay with strip bonds issued by the federal or provincial governments.

We also tend to steer investors who wish to utilize this strategy to use one or more mutual funds for the equity portion of the portfolio. The reason is one of logistics: an investor wanting to use this strategy is likely so drawn by the absolute preservation of capital offered. Our experience is that this same investor does not wish to engage in individual stock selection, preferring instead to leave the day-to-day buying and selling decisions to one or more professional portfolio managers.

This strategy is most suitable for RRSP accounts because the interest that compounds over the years will not have to be declared on an annual income tax return. Present tax laws state that interest earned on strip bonds must be reported (and tax paid) every year, even though you may not have received a payment. It is for this reason that someone who holds strip bonds outside an RRSP is considered to have a cash-flow-negative investment, and that strip bonds are best held in RRSPs. For more information on strip bonds, please refer to Chapter 7, Show Me the Money.

Income Cassoulet: *A unique blend of tastes and textures pairing rich, earthy bonds with succulent equities to produce a consistent, harmonious yield. Served with a light drizzle of cash.*

This strategy is best utilized by investors in need of a stable income stream from their portfolios. It's a strategy that is right at home in a RRIF account. The cash component acts like a reservoir, drawn down as the investor requires income and replenished as the investments generate yield. The equity portion of this strategy should lean toward income-generating equities, which could include REITs, income trusts, preferred shares, dividend funds or common stock of companies with a reputation for stable—or better yet, rising—dividends.

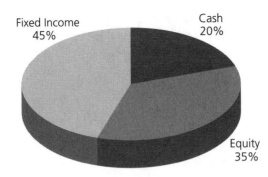

Balanced Bouillabaisse: *An enticing melange of succulent, growing companies matched with a satisfying assortment of slowly maturing bonds and topped with a dollop of cash.*

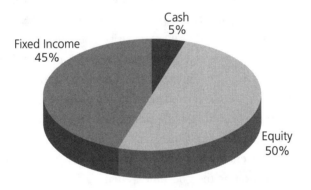

This is another example of an asset allocation strategy well suited to RRSP accounts. The interest earned on the fixed-income and cash components can gather free of the burden of an annual tax bill if held inside a registered account. Investors who wish to achieve some degree of growth in their RRSPs can realize growth from the prescribed equity exposure, while the stabilizing influence of the fixed-income element will help take off the rough edges as the market manoeuvres through inevitable peaks and valleys. The small but essential cash component is included to provide both an additional stabilizing influence and liquidity with which to capitalize on market declines.

Growth Mixed Grill: *Succulent morsels of well-aged equities grown slowly to perfection. Served with a side of fixed income and cash slaw.*

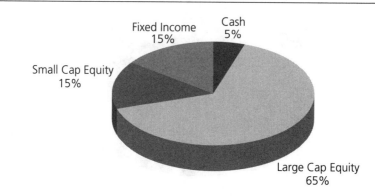

Fixed Income 15% · Cash 5% · Small Cap Equity 15% · Large Cap Equity 65%

The typical investor for this asset allocation strategy is seeking long-term growth, yet is not prepared to risk significant capital loss. The equities selected for this portfolio will more often than not tend to be large, established companies, yet there is a smattering of small-cap equities to provide the opportunity for more accelerated growth. The dominant security selection theme for equities in this portfolio should be value (see the next section for details); it can be easily constructed using individual equities (where sufficient capital exists; we suggest no less than $100,000), exchange traded funds, investment counsellor mandates (again, where minimum asset thresholds are met) or mutual funds.

Fixed income and cash once again play a role, albeit a diminished one, of providing liquidity to enable the growth-oriented investor to take advantage of bargains in the market as they become available. The cash and fixed-income segments should be replenished with profits taken on excessively large, growing positions.

Aggressive Growth Soufflé: *A melange of large cap, growth companies spiked with a profusion of small cap delicacies, topping with a light drizzle of cash and short-term bonds.*

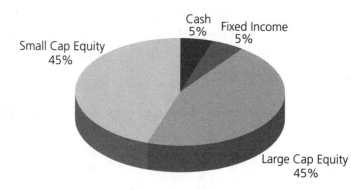

Cash 5% · Fixed Income 5% · Small Cap Equity 45% · Large Cap Equity 45%

Just as a cook preparing a soufflé may have a nightmare that the carefully crafted dish will fall before serving, the investor fears that his or her carefully crafted portfolio will suffer a similar fate leading to financial hardship. This allocation strategy is designed for an investor who is seeking to maximize his or her growth potential, and is prepared to withstand some degree of capital loss in the quest for growth. The small cash and fixed-income weightings are intended to provide liquidity in the event of a decline in market prices for selected equities, allowing the investor to capitalize on attractive prices. As a result, the 5% weighting in fixed income should be kept to fairly short maturities. The equity holdings under this strategy would tend to focus more on the growth method of security selection than on the value approach, which we delve into next.

Large Cap vs. Small Cap

The "cap" in this instance has nothing to do with headgear but rather with the size of a corporation as measured by its market capitalization. In Canada, a small-capitalization firm is generally regarded as a company with a market capitalization of less than $250 million. In the United States, the bar is much higher. Small cap stocks in the United States are shares of companies with a market capitalization of under $500 million.

GROWTH VS. VALUE

Selecting securities for the equity portion of portfolios brings investors face to face with the choice of taking either a value approach or a growth approach. Most mutual fund managers do just this, qualifying themselves as either growth or value-style fund managers. Successful investors know that matching equal parts of growth and value funds in a portfolio is one way to add another layer of diversification to the equity portion.

The value style of stock selection has been made famous by legendary portfolio managers such as Sir John Templeton and Warren Buffett. Simply put, it means seeking out stocks that are trading for less than their intrinsic value. In other words, value investors are trying to buy a dollar for seventy-five cents. Benjamin Graham (once again, related to Michael only in spirit) saw underpriced securities as investments providing a margin of safety. Similarly, Warren Buffett has always liked a moat of safety around his investments. For risk-sensitive investors, stocks chosen through the value method of security selection are usually the most appropriate choices.

An investor who focuses on the growth method of stock selection is on the lookout for companies with the capability of growing their earnings at a pace fast enough to warrant a rise in the share price. This style of manager is typically less concerned with valuation than with putting growth funds into use in portfolios where investors have an above-average tolerance for risk.

In addition, there is a class of asset managers who are considered hybrids. These exotic birds refer to themselves as GARP (growth at a reasonable price) managers. Their definition of reasonable is somewhat subjective, and can vary quite significantly from one manager to the next. If you are considering the addition of a GARP style of mutual fund in your portfolio, take a look at the top holdings of the fund. That, together with an examination of the degree of volatility of the fund's unit price over a span of several years, will give you some insight into whether or not the fund fits your comfort level and needs.

AN OUNCE OF PREVENTION...

The highly disciplined application of strategic asset allocation helps all of us to avoid that natural human tendency of wanting to load up our portfolios with equities when stock indexes are in full flight, and to rush to cash in times of market turmoil. The inclination to fall victim to our own emotions of fear and greed can be found at the root of most, if not all, wounded portfolios.

Taking the time to work through an asset allocation strategy custom-tailored to your own unique needs before selecting investments will go a long way toward making more rational, less emotional investment decisions. You should also remember to include direction on both when and how to rebalance your portfolio, so that the delicate balance between risk and reward that you worked so hard to achieve at the outset of the investment process is not thrown into disarray by a rapidly appreciating or depreciating security.

CHAPTER 7

Show Me the Money

Investing for Income

Several years ago Holiday Inn had a marketing slogan that promised "no surprises." This is exactly what you should be striving for if you are one of the millions of fully or partially retired Canadians who require an income from their portfolio. The income stream generated by your investments should be reliable and highly predictable. Do not rely on peeling off rising market values as a substitute for an income stream. Capital appreciation should come from growth investments such as stocks or stock-based mutual funds. In order to have a reliable income stream generated by your investments, turn to investment vehicles whose primary purpose is generating a steady, reliable stream of income. To do otherwise is a little like having a wild bucking bronco from the Calgary Stampede brought in to give pony rides at a children's birthday party.

GIVE ME A BRAKE!

Investing for income is often viewed as the domain of widows and orphans. This view is grossly misleading. Even the most aggressive growth investor will at various points in time have a need to place some portion of their portfolio in fixed-income investments. A portfolio with no fixed-income representation is like a car with no brakes. In this chapter, we will introduce you to securities and strategies that can be used to generate an income, yet can also be used where appropriate as risk management tools.

LOANING AND OWNING

Loaning and owning are the two components that define investing. Loaning is contractual and finite. Owning is entrepreneurial and residual. To put it another way, bonds, GICs and most other fixed-income instruments are, for the most part, a case of what you see is what you get. You are lending your money to the issuer. The bond (or GIC, etc.) is in effect an IOU from the issuer to pay back your money at a specific point in the future, and to pay you a prescribed rate of interest in consideration for having the use of your money. This is the essence of fixed-income investing.

Equities are another matter altogether. Buying shares in a corporation means that you have taken an ownership stake in the company. You have become an owner rather than a loaner. Here there is no maturity date, no guarantees on a return of your capital. Your earnings can be much greater or much less than the return on a comparable size fixed-income investment. It all depends on the success of the company in turning a profit. We'll focus on the owning aspect of investing in the next chapter. In this chapter, our focus will remain primarily on the loaning side of the equation, but we will occasionally cross over into the owning side as it pertains to income-generating equities such as income trusts and preferred shares.

RISKS AND REWARDS

Like equities, fixed-income securities can have "good" or "bad" prices during their income-generating lives to maturity. Also like equities, there will be times when they represent exceptional investment value, and others when they are overpriced and need to be sold, trimmed or best avoided. Michael vividly remembers the mid-1980s when bond yields were in the mid-teens and real (after-inflation) yields were of a magnitude seldom seen; in other words, bonds were at a stage where their returns could no longer be ignored. There are risks associated with bond investing too. Like equities, there can be no escaping *en passant* investment risk, whether direct or indirect.

CREDIT RISK

Directly, there is the risk of the lender being unable to meet interest and repayment commitments. It's a risk that can inflict considerable damage on portfolios. More recently, investors who lent their precious savings to household names such as Air

Canada, Confederation Life, Royal Trustco and Stelco can ruefully testify to what credit risk can come to mean.

Occasionally, credit worthiness can go wrong even at the highest level. An irony of history records Alberta as the last Canadian province to have defaulted on its debts—back in the "dirty" 1930s. A fairly recent example of how even the debt of a sovereign nation can be hurtful is Argentina, where damaged creditors eventually agreed to swap U.S.$102 billion of that country's bad debt for U.S.$25 billion of new bonds—the largest restructuring in history. The cardinal rule of knowing what you are investing in applies as much to fixed income as it does to equities.

Fortunately, today's debt markets are blessed with skilled experts like Standard & Poor's Rating Services, Canadian Bond Rating Service and Dominion Bond Rating Service who provide valuable assistance in grading credit risk. Their expertise should be a mandatory first step in checking the quality of the fixed-income investments being considered. We make a point of investing in bonds (or equivalent) with an "A" or "1" rating, and only rarely make exceptions with "B" or "2"-rated bonds. We steadfastly ignore debt instruments with lower ratings, or no ratings at all. No matter how enticing the yield, we prefer to stay away from inferior credit ratings. Our belief is that if the fixed-income element of your portfolio is destined to be the safe money, you don't want to obscure its purpose by taking on heightened risk. Bond traders have a name for investors who scrounge through the markets in search of above-average yields: yield pigs. There is also a quaint little aphorism that every bond trader has committed to memory by the end of their first day on the job that describes the ultimate fate of yield pigs: *Bulls make money. Bears make money. Pigs get slaughtered!* Fixed-income investing involves enough risks anyway; credit risk just isn't worth it—not at any price.

INTEREST-RATE RISK AND THE INVERSE RELATIONSHIP

Over the lifespan of fixed-income investments, the twin risks of rising interest rates and inflation can take their toll on the market price of an investment despite eventual repayment at par (assuming a good credit rating).

Rising interest rates diminish the value of existing bonds in the market. As the price of a bond declines, the yield offered to a potential purchaser increases. The faster interest rates rise, the more dramatic the drop in a given bond's price until the yield offered reflects the "going rate" of the day. The opposite occurs when interest rates drop. Bond prices appreciate, sending yields lower to reflect, once again, the prevailing yield of the day.

This phenomenon of bond prices falling when interest rates rise and rising when rates fall is what is known as fixed-income securities' unique *inverse relationship* with interest rates. All things being equal, the longer into the future the maturity date of a bond, the more susceptible it will be to price fluctuations from changing interest rates.

For this reason, it is a good idea to keep your bond maturities fairly short if you are expecting interest rates to rise in the near term. If, however, your expectation is for a steep drop in lending rates, the strategy then shifts to extending the average term to maturity in the fixed-income portion of your portfolio. This will enable you to lock in today's soon-to-be-high rates for as long as possible, and offer a boost to the market value of your portfolio as the bonds appreciate. If you learn nothing else from reading this chapter, let it be the concept of the inverse relationship between fixed-income securities and interest rates. Keeping this front and centre in your thinking will dramatically improve your results as a fixed-income investor.

The temptation for some investors is to trade bonds and other fixed-income securities for quick profits despite the interest-rate risk, in a manner not dissimilar to what day traders do with equities. Short-term trading of any kind is not for the faint of heart, and is in the overwhelming majority of instances best left to qualified professionals.

THE RISING COST OF LIVING

Inflation eats away at the purchasing power of the fixed interest payments as they are received over the life of a bond. As a result, the return that really counts is the "real" return; that is, what remains after deducting the rate of inflation from the current yield. Real returns can fluctuate widely, as the following chart illustrates.

Government of Canada 10-Year Bond Yields
– Actual & Real Returns, 1990 – Mid-2005

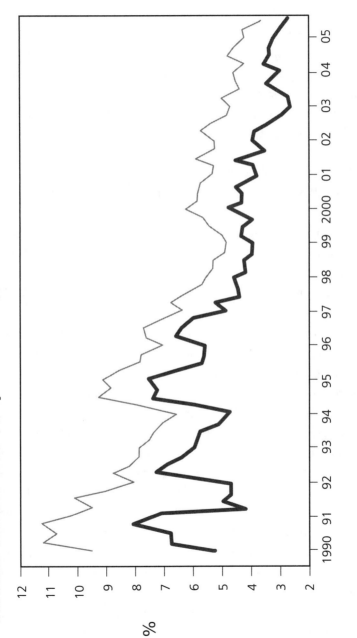

Note: Actual yield (thin line) at end of quarter, real yield (thick line) after deducting CPI y/y %.
Sources: Bloomberg L.P., Merrill Lynch Canada

Over time the true, inflation-adjusted lending rate at which one can lend in meaningful terms emerges at about 4%. Above this historical level of real return, bonds and equivalent fixed-income instruments offer excellent, sometimes even outstanding, value. Below this level, warning flags should begin to fly. If real returns fall to zero or turn negative and remedial portfolio action hasn't been taken, the results can be very sobering. Remedial action would, in this instance, include shortening the average term to maturity in the fixed-income section of your portfolio and/or raising the cash/cash equivalency levels (money market funds, Treasury bills, banker's acceptances, etc.). This has the effect of defending against the risk to the value of your portfolio brought on by rising interest rates.

LESSONS OF HISTORY

In the early 1980s, when our story on the need for *Portfolio First Aid* begins, there didn't seem to be any refuge in either stocks or bonds from raging double-digit inflation and soaring interest rates. Who could imagine the rates at which the Canadian banks lent to their prime customers peaking at just under 20%, or the yields on long-term Government of Canada bonds approximating 18%? Michael even remembers a Canada Savings Bond issue with a 16% yield selling poorly. With the benefit of hindsight we can only shake our heads and say, "What incredible bargains!" The widespread view of the time was that interest rates were headed still higher. Who would want to buy at 16% or 18% when you believed you would soon be able to get 20%?

"Bonds, the buy of the generation" was the message that Michael, then the strategist at Dominion Securities Ames, and fellow research director Peter McMullin took across the country in the first half of 1982. It was a tough sell in shell-shocked markets. Michael remembers, in particular, a presentation in Calgary where oil and gas offered seemingly easy profits and home prices were on the rise. Both were deemed worthier investment alternatives than bonds. No one cared much for what Michael and Peter had to say at the time, even though the real returns on bonds were starting to become too compelling to ignore. About that time real rates were beginning a climb that would take them to a stratospheric 8% and beyond. One year later, the reception in Calgary was altogether different.

Nominal bond yields remained in a double-digit to mid-teen range, and real rates at exceptionally attractive historical levels, right up until the great stock market crash of October 1987. It was only then that frenzied investors sought refuge in the bond markets, and the nominal yields on mid- to long-term Government of Canada bonds finally fell below 10%.

It was in the early 1980s that the high-interest-rate medicine of central bankers Paul Volcker in the U.S. and Gerald Bouey in Canada began having its desired effect. As inflation proxied by the Consumer Price Index (CPI) began subsiding, bonds (and equivalents) became ever-better investment bargains. When this realization dawned on previously skeptical markets, the prices of bond issues paying double-digit interest rates surged. Looking back, what once-in-a-lifetime bargains, and how bonds bought throughout that period were to boost overall portfolio returns for years to come!

Two decades later, the opposite was true when interest rates began a steep descent and accompanying bond yields were to experience another extreme. In 2003–2004, the nominal yields on benchmark long-term Government of Canada bonds fell to between 4% to 5%, their lowest levels in over 40 years. Unbelievably, Michael could once again use his 1960s yield book, which tops out at 6%. In the bond markets, the prices of outstanding issues soared as upward adjustments brought their yields into prevailing market line. Increasingly, good-credit bond prices exceeded their maturity values. This in turn meant bond prices carrying an element of eventual capital loss. Inflation was falling as well and real returns remained positive, though far less than history's time-proven inflation-adjusted 4%.

Herein lay another extreme element of interest rate risk. When real returns drop to the 2% area, bonds that were once bargains become progressively overpriced and detract from overall portfolio performance. This remains today's challenge in the face of central bank policies of gradual upward adjustment in the interest rates they administer, and as market rates and yields follow suit. It's an investment challenge to be prudently dealt with.

FIXED-INCOME STRATEGIES

The fact that bonds are repayable at maturity reflects increasingly in their market prices the closer they get to maturity. Certainty of principal repayment (assuming credit worthiness) also means interest-rate risk and volatility can be hedged against along the way. The strategies to do so are many and can sometimes be quite complex. We covered the most frequently used strategy earlier when we examined the inverse relationship between bond values and interest rates.

BONDS AND LADDERS

The simplest means of protecting your portfolio against the shifting fortunes of rising and falling interest rates is by staggering the maturities of your bonds. This is where you have bond maturities occurring at regular intervals into the future. A bond ladder has the advantage of giving built-in protection against both interest-rate scenarios. If rates are set to rise, the shortest term-to-maturity bonds in the ladder can be reinvested at maturity into longer-dated and presumably higher-yield bonds in an act that bears some resemblance to a game of leapfrog. If rates are on the decline, the bonds out at the long end of the ladder will appreciate in value and help to preserve the overall value of the ladder.

When constructing a bond ladder, we like to divide the total dollar value of the fixed-income component of the portfolio by 10. We then look for bonds (or related debt equivalents) of a more or less equal amount maturing successively in each of the 10 years from whatever date the ladder begins. As each bond matures, the proceeds can be reinvested in another 10-year maturity, thereby repeatedly adding new rungs to what becomes a perpetual ladder.

ARNOLD SCHWARZENEGGER'S FAVOURITE: THE BARBELL STRATEGY

If an investor's portfolio does not contain enough capital to build a proper bond ladder, a sensible alternative is to invest half the fixed-income section of the portfolio in shorter-term securities and the other half in longer-term maturities. This is what is known as a barbell strategy. This strategy can be especially opportune when the yield curve is flattening and there is no great advantage to leaning one way or the other, or when there are insufficient funds to build a proper ladder.

MONTHLY INCOME PORTFOLIOS

Bonds that pay their interest out to investors, and not all do, generally make their payments every six months. For an investor looking for a reliable, consistent income stream from their investments, getting paid only twice per year can be inconvenient. To counter this, build a ladder made of at least six bonds with successive annual maturities, but with each paying their semi-annual interest in different months (e.g., January–July, February–August, March–September and so on). This way, the bond section of a portfolio can be made to generate income every month of the year, as illustrated in the accompanying example from Michael's files of the mid-1990s.

Monthly Income Bond Portfolio
Cash Flow on $97,388 Principal Investment

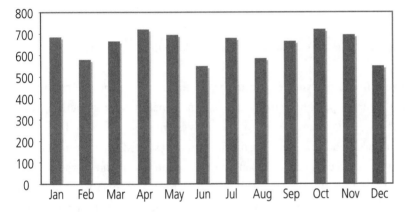

Monthly Income Bond Portfolio

Issuer	Value	Rating*	Coupon	Maturity	Price	Cost**
CMHC	$14,000	AAA	8.25%	Aug. '99	$104.45	$14,623
CMHC	15,000	AAA	8.80	Mar. '00	106.95	16,043
Canada	15,000	AAA	9.50	Oct. '01	111.30	16,695
British Columbia	15,000	AA	9.00	Jan. '02	108.05	16,208
Alberta	18,000	AA	7.75	May '03	101.00	18,180
Alberta	17,000	AA	6.38	Jun. '04	92.00	15,640
	$94,000					$97,389

Annual Income $ 7,729 ***
Weighted Term 6.5 years
Weighted Yield 7.32%

*By DBRS
**As of June 23, 1995; excluding accrued interest
***In monthly payments ranging from $542 to $713

Ladders like these assure income while smoothing out interest-rate risk. They also average out volatility and keep current the principal value of the fixed-income section of portfolios. Because bond prices customarily build in a premium to compensate for inflation, the continuous adding of new maturities to the ladder automatically provides an element of inflation protection. By dividing the fixed-income section into equal amounts over a range of maturities, you can avoid the hazards of forecasting future interest rates—never an easy task at the best of times.

A BEVY OF BONDS TO CHOOSE FROM
Strip Bonds

For investors who do not yet need to derive an income from their portfolio, the semi-annual interest payments from bonds can sometimes be something of a nuisance. Often the payments in and of themselves are too small to roll over into another bond, or to add to a stock position. If the investment account in question is an RRSP, taking the cash out and spending it is not an option due to the onerous tax consequences. Many investors will allow the interest payments to accumulate as part of the cash reserve in their portfolio, but what do you do when that reservoir of cash is brimming over? Strip bonds (introduced in the *Portfolio First Aid* Café Menu last chapter) are frequently the answer.

Strip bonds derive their name from the manner in which they are conceived. They are existing federal, provincial, municipal and sometimes even corporate bonds that have been separated into their component parts of interest payments and principal payments. These components are then made available to investors as individual securities. Strip bonds act a little like a compound GIC in that no interest is actually paid out until maturity. Strip bond prices, like the price of all bonds, depend on current interest rate levels and can vary from day to day. Unlike more traditional fixed-income investments, these bonds are always priced below par. The interest earned on a strip bond is the difference between the discounted price and the bond's matured value of par (100 cents on the dollar).

Strip bonds can be sold prior to their maturity date, but like any other type of fixed-income investment, the price you receive will be a reflection of prevailing interest rates. This can work either for you or against you. Our advice to clients has always been to never buy a strip bond, or any bond at all for that matter, with a maturity that is longer than you are prepared to hold the bond.

The folks at the Canada Revenue Agency have determined in their infinite wisdom that the difference between the purchase value and the maturity value of a strip bond constitutes accrued interest. As such, if you hold strip bonds in a non-registered investment account, the amount of interest that you are deemed to have earned in a given year must be reported on your income tax return. This creates a negative cash flow situation because you will be forced to pay tax on income that you have not yet received. It is for this reason that we recommend strip bonds be used primarily for RRSP accounts.

Convertible Debentures

Debentures are debt instruments offered by corporations. Unlike a bond, a debenture is not secured by any mortgage or any other lien on specific assets of the issuer. The line between bonds and debentures often gets blurred by investors who refer to all long-term debt obligations as bonds.

Convertible debentures offer the income-producing qualities of a bond and the capital appreciation potential of an equity. A convertible debenture offers the holder, for a predetermined period of time, the right to convert the debenture to a specific number of common shares at a specified price. This conversion right is valuable if the underlying stock escalates in value, but like the purchase of a convertible roadster, this feature comes at a cost. Issuers can usually price convertible debentures with a yield that is slightly below that of a comparable regular bond or debenture since the convertible has the capital gain potential that other fixed-income investments do not have.

Real Return Bonds

One way to protect against inflation is to invest in real return bonds. Also called inflation-protected bonds, real return bonds have the unique feature of the issuer annually raising the principal on repayment by the previous year's rate of inflation. Unfortunately, the Canadian market in these bonds is mostly limited to a few series of Government of Canada bonds. Even then, however, real return bonds can become over- or underpriced, and as such there are accompanying risks.

Corporate Bonds

Often, an investor who wishes to boost the overall yield on the fixed-income portion of his or her portfolio will look to the bonds of major corporations as the solution. This is a reasonable prospect, yet it is also one that can potentially turn up the risk profile of the overall portfolio by several degrees. We have witnessed situations where investors have bought the bonds of a company in distress, attracted to a yield that sits considerably higher than that of comparable term-to-maturity bonds. This is an act that is very similar to "catching a falling knife," which we described in Chapter 2. Great care must be taken in the selection of corporate bonds to make sure you have not bought an empty promise. Just as you would lend money to your brother-in-law only if you were confident he could eventually repay the loan, so too with corporate bonds. Don't buy a company's bonds if you are not confident of its ability to make payments of principal and interest to you. This is where the debt-rating agencies can be a real life saver. Our rule of thumb is that we will not buy the debt of any company if we would not gladly purchase its stock.

Never forget the relationship between risk and reward. The higher the yield, the greater the risk. Fortunately, there are a large variety of good-quality bonds available from many of the world's greatest corporations that can really add an enticing dimension to a fixed-income strategy. Please see Chapter 9 for more information on debt ratings. If there is research available on the stock of the company, it's a good idea to read it so you can gain further insight into the company and be able to spot debt-related problems before they become catastrophic.

Many corporate bond issues have a call feature that enables the company, under certain predetermined conditions, to call in bonds for redemption prior to maturity. This is a little like having the ability to renegotiate your mortgage well before maturity if interest rates were to drop. In the corporate world, these call features enable a company to reissue debt at more favourable terms to the issuer if market conditions permit.

For the holder (that would be you), this presents a problem in that the highly attractive yield that you may have become quite accustomed to receiving disappears when the bond in question is called. You may be forced by the exercising of the call feature to reinvest your money at a much less favourable yield; this is known as reinvestment risk. For investors are who reliant on a stable income stream from their portfolios, the consequences can be lifestyle altering. If you are going to invest in corporate bonds with a call feature, your best defence is to have all of the facts before you.

The bond market and, by extension, bond pricing tend to be anticipatory by nature. That means that bond prices are continually readjusted to reflect potential future events. When shopping for corporate bonds, find out first if the bond you are interested in has a call feature. If it does, take a look at the bond's yield to call, not its yield to maturity. If the bond has multiple call dates, focus on the yield to the first call date. Operating under the assumption that a bond with a call feature is going to be called away at the first opportunity, and focusing on the yield to that call date, leaves little room for unpleasant surprises.

PLAYING THE YIELD CURVE

For those who nevertheless want to run the interest-rate gauntlet and capitalize on bond market swings, the ladder of maturities can be lengthened or shortened according to their forecasts. If you foresee rising rates, shorten the ladder of maturities; if you expect falling rates, lock in existing yield by extending term and adding more rungs to the ladder. What is then effectively being sought is the point in time where the advantage along the yield curve is greatest.

What Is the Yield Curve?

The yield curve is a curve that can be readily drawn by connecting the dots reflecting different maturities, all the way from 30 days to 30 years. It's also a curve regularly shown and updated in most financial newspapers. Sometimes ongoing interest rate and yield changes have a see-saw effect; if rates go up at the short end of the yield curve, they go down at the long end. Other times there are undulating patterns because some yields change less or more than others, and there is more relative advantage in one part of the yield curve than in another.

Of great importance to fixed-income investors is the overall slope, or steepness, of the yield curve, which helps them determine how adventurous or conservative they need to be.

When short rates and yields are higher than long yields, the yield curve is said to have an inverted slope. An inverted yield curve is generally regarded as a signal of pending economic slowdown. This is what happened in the early 1980s when central bankers dramatically raised interest rates to contain inflation and bonds became the irresistible bargains that were referred to earlier in this chapter.

Warren Buffett once famously wrote that there are times when "an absence of activity is not necessarily an indication of an absence of intelligence." We couldn't agree more. There is plenty of comfort in effectively keeping your fixed-income component waiting on the sidelines in the form of short-term instruments like 90-day government Treasury bills, a strategy that would have served all investors well in the early 1980s when interest rates were in an astonishingly rapid ascent. The same is true when the yield curve is flat, as happened in the early 2000s when the returns obtainable on all maturities, short and long, were essentially the same. At times like this, why reach out when you can comfortably sit and wait?

Realize, however, that when long yields are higher than short rates and the yield curve has a positive slope to it, the advantage becomes progressively greater, and waiting on the sidelines generally isn't the best idea.

BOND FUNDS

One of the oldest and probably corniest jokes on Bay Street concerns bond fund managers. We would be remiss in our professional duties if we did not take a moment to pass this comedic gem on to you.

What's the difference between a bond and a bond fund manager?

The bond will eventually mature!

Okay, that's enough fun and hilarity for now. Sit up straight, everyone, as we enter into the buttoned-down world of bond funds.

Bond funds are mutual funds that allow an investor to own a professionally managed portfolio of fixed-income securities. They are, in our view, ideally suited for the novice investor who has not yet amassed enough capital to build his or her own selection of fixed-income investments. We are defining "enough" in this instance as a fixed-income portfolio component of at least $50,000.

For those who do have "enough," our preference, more often than not, is to bypass bond funds in favour of owning bonds and other fixed-income securities directly. We mean no disrespect to bond fund managers who work very hard on behalf of their unit holders and the majority of whom are exceptionally bright, energetic professionals doing their job. The problem as we see it is that, with few exceptions, most bond funds are not able to earn enough additional return over that of a simple bond portfolio to justify the underlying management expenses that are borne by the unit holder. As if that weren't enough, a significant number of the bond funds monitored by the respected tracking agency Morningstar have 10-year performance track records that fall below the widely recognized fixed-income benchmark, the Scotia Capital Universe Bond Index.

Of course, there are special situations where the cool head and unique expertise of a portfolio manager can turn out to be preferential to going it alone. The complexities of international currencies and knowledge of foreign debt ratings make a strong case for the use of a global bond fund manager. A similar argument can be made when it comes to high-yield corporate bonds. Often, corporations that offer exceptionally high yields on their debt securities are compelled to do so by circumstances such as poor debt ratings, high debt-to-equity ratios or precarious business conditions such as the loss of a major customer. It is for all of these reasons, and more, that an investor would turn to a qualified portfolio manager for the day-to-day monitoring and quality control of high-yield bonds.

INCOME-GENERATING EQUITIES

The ultimate extension of term is into equities, which Michael facetiously refers to as perpetual bonds (never maturing) with floating rates of (dividend) return. It's because of these qualities that a steeply positive yield curve can effectively inhibit a bear market in equities by obliging investors to reach ever further out— and ultimately into equities—for desirable yield and total return. This need was undoubtedly a factor in the bull market in equities that began taking hold over the winter of 2002–2003 when central bank and related interest rates began falling to 40-year lows, long bond yields fell in tandem and income returns in portfolios came under inexorable pressure.

This exceptional fall in interest rates and yields brought a welcome reminder that investing for income should also encompass dividend-paying stocks. Traditionally, these have been utility-type stocks known for their relatively high dividend payouts. In recent years, however, dividends have taken on a whole new importance as a rising source of income. It's a topic we'll pick up on in the next chapter, but we will note at this stage that investing for income can include much more than debt securities.

INCOME TRUSTS

This ode to bonds and other fixed-income investing would not be complete without including income trusts, a largely Canadian phenomenon that has bridged the developing income gap with great effect for yield-starved investors willing to forgo the security of capital offered by bonds in at least a fraction of their portfolio.

"Income trusts are just stocks, but with a yield advantage," says Ira Gluskin of Gluskin Sheff & Associates, one of the foremost advocates and users of income trusts. Income trusts began to receive widespread attention in the mid-1990s and have swept yield-hungry Canadian investment markets with an ever-expanding array of choices.

There are three main breeds of income trusts:

- **Royalty trusts** make payments to investors on the basis of royalties earned on producing oil and gas properties owned or leased by the trust. Examples include Arc Energy Trust and Pengrowth Energy Fund.
- **Income trusts** are usually tied to some form of operating company. One of Canada's largest income trusts, Yellow Pages Income Fund, generates income for unit holders from the revenue earned on the famous Yellow Pages directories. There are also pipeline and utility income trusts that earn steady cash flow from their operations. This type of trust is popular for the high level of predictability to their cash flow. It is precisely because of this, however, that pipeline- and utility-based income trusts tend to have a greater sensitivity to interest-rate fluctuations than business-based trusts. Examples of pipeline and utility trusts include Pembina Pipeline Income Fund and TransCanada Power.
- **Real estate income trusts (REITS)** are, as the name implies, income trusts built around income-producing real estate, such as shopping centres, retirement homes, hotels, etc. Some of the more widely known REITs in Canada include RioCan (shopping centres), CHIP REIT (hotels) and Retirement Residences Real Estate Investment Trust (just try to guess what that is into).

The income trust structure lends itself best to mature companies readily able to disburse rather than retain the bulk of their earnings. It's a structure that also lends itself to companies with asset bases capable of generating revenue and earnings over an extended period of time.

The unique structure of income trusts allows them to avoid the payment of income tax at the corporate level by regularly passing on the income flowing through them to unit holders. In Canada, the era of low interest rates saw income trusts becoming a steady source of income that in some cases could provide yields running into double digits. Not only did they become immensely popular with cash-hungry retail investors, but also with non-taxable foundations, charitable institutions, pension and trusteed funds.

Such has been their growth from a handful of initial oil and gas trusts in the mid-1990s that the income trust sector of the Canadian investment market now numbers approximately 200 trusts listed on the Toronto Stock Exchange—and continuously counting. At the time of writing, the collective market capitalization of the income trust market is in the order of C$120 billion, or about 8% of the total Toronto Stock Exchange market capitalization. So important (and legitimate) have these trusts become that they are in the process of being added to the S&P/TSX Composite Index as a separate subsection. Soon, a small selection of the country's largest, most actively traded income trusts and REITs will be included in the Index. This means greater acceptance with institutional investors managing funds that are obliged to pattern their investing off this benchmark index.

Their unique and complex structure means that investing in income trusts, just like all other investments, requires due diligence. In essence, they are trusts that conduct their own investing through a combination of shares in an operating company (the underlying business) and high-interest loans to the same company. The interest on these loans is designed to eliminate profits in the operating company and flow that income to the trust, which, in turn, passes it and dividends received from the operating company through to its unit holders who must then face the tax consequences of the income received.

In this way, the double taxation of profits (at the company level and on dividends paid to shareholders) is avoided. The flow-through income trust structure means income that would otherwise be taxed twice now being taxed just once. This means that income received from income trust units held in a non-registered account is often taxed at a lower (personal) rate. In addition, interest income from bonds is fully taxable, sometimes even before it is received (see strip bonds). Often the income from an income trust includes a return of capital element in which the tax is deferred as it will be deemed to be part of the capital gain when the units are disposed of at a later date.

When income trust units are held in RRSPs, RRIFs and RPPs (Registered Pension Plans), tax is deferred until eventual payout to plan and fund participants. When held in charitable funds with an approved registration, income trust units essentially provide investment income free of tax. No matter what type of account structure you choose for holding income trust units, there is a potentially significant cumulative tax advantage over the common corporate structure, which helps to explain their enormous popularity in a highly-taxed Canada.

This type of investment is not without risks. Rising interest rates, deteriorating underlying commodity prices and changing business fundamentals are three of the most significant risks of which income trust investors must be cognizant. It is for this reason that income trust unit holders must be continuously evaluating the state of their income trust holdings, keeping a watch for both internal risks (increasing levels of debt, rising costs, falling sales) and the aforementioned external risks.

Income trusts are required to report financial results on a quarterly basis just like their common share cousins. These quarterly reports and the accompanying research analyst reports offer an ideal opportunity for follow-up by either you or your advisor.

The sheer, widespread popularity of income trusts today leaves some market commentators worried. Surging demand has raised many income trust unit prices, reducing their prospective yields to levels where their income-generating advantage is nowhere near as great as when many of the trusts first came to market. Selectivity is of paramount importance, since no two income trusts are identical. Each must be judged on its own merits. With each issue, the first question an investor should ask is how sustainable are the earnings that will support the distributions to unit holders.

The word "trust" denotes an investment of paramount quality, and of regular, reliable income distribution. Because of the attendant risks, income trusts should never replace bonds and other debt-related securities in the fixed-income section of portfolios. Instead, they should be looked on as a good accompaniment to fixed-income investments.

We've recommended and used income trusts to telling effect. Barring any significant changes in the tax treatment of income trusts, we will continue to do so. They can be a tremendous addition to a portfolio that is mandated to provide income.

PREFERRED SHARES

Preferred shares are a little different from their common share cousins. Before a company can make a dividend to common shareholders, holders of preferred shares must receive their dividends. Furthermore, the dividends they must pay are usually cumulative, which means that any missed dividend payments must be made good before a common shareholder gets his or her turn. From a security standpoint, in the event of a company's bankruptcy, preferred shareholders rank after all creditors but ahead of common shareholders for a claim on the assets of the company.

Investors buy preferred shares for what most often is a stable stream of dividend income. Most preferred share issues pay a fixed dividend. If the dividends are paid by a tax-paying Canadian corporation, the dividend tax credit kicks in.

The dividend tax credit is a reduction in the amount of tax a shareholder must pay on the dividends received from Canadian tax-paying corporations. The purpose of the tax credit is to partially offset the effect of double taxation. The earnings that the company generated in order to pay dividends were first taxed at the corporate level. To have these same dollars taxed once they reach the shareholder without offering at least some degree of relief truly would be a double whammy. All of this is irrelevant if you were to hold preferred shares inside an RRSP or RRIF account because the income generated by investments held in these types of accounts are not taxed; only capital that is removed from the accounts is subject to tax. As such, the dividend tax credit would not apply under this situation.

The Many Different Breeds of Preferred Shares

These are among the more common breeds of preferred share issues that you are likely to encounter in the market.

Perpetual Preferred Shares

Commonly known as straight preferreds, this type of share pays a fixed rate of dividend. Price changes are primarily the result of interest-rate fluctuations. Perpetual preferreds do not have a maturity date, but do carry a redemption date. This redemption date is the time at which the issuer can call the issue in for redemption. Redemption is generally not mandatory on the part of the issuer.

Retractable Preferred Shares

Although most preferred share issues are redeemable, there is no guarantee that a call feature will be exercised by the issuer. A retractable preferred will provide the investor with the ability (under certain predetermined conditions) to force the company to redeem the issue. If a retraction feature expires unutilized, the shares become perpetual preferreds.

Soft Retractable Preferred Shares

This is a feature found with retractable preferred share issues, in which the redemption value could be paid either in cash or in common stock of the company. The choice is up to the issuer.

As is the case with fixed-income investments, credit quality is a highly important consideration when selecting preferred shares. For us, suitable preferred shares must have a rating of Pfd1 or Pfd2 from the Dominion Bond Rating Service or a similar rating from one of the other major rating agencies such as Standard & Poor's.

Many of the risks associated with fixed-income investments apply equally to preferred shares. Such risks include:

- interest rate risk
- call risk
- credit risk
- liquidity risk

Interest Rate Risk

Just as bonds have an inverse relationship with interest rates, so too do most preferred share issues. This may not be much of a concern for long-term, buy-and-hold investors who are less concerned about fluctuations in market value and more concerned about stability of income. However, for the investor with a shorter time horizon (e.g., less than five years), fluctuations in value can be a significant concern.

Generally, preferred share issues with higher-than-average yields tend to be less sensitive to interest-rate fluctuations. Yet one does have to question why an issuer is offering such a high yield in the first place. With preferred issues with very high yields, interest-rate sensitivity may turn out to be the least of your concerns; instead, it could be solvency that is the overriding risk. Issues that are close to their call date also tend to display less-than-average interest-rate sensitivity.

Call Risk

Many preferred share issues on the market today have call provisions attached to them. This is wonderful for the issuer because the call provision affords a great degree of flexibility, but it is usually not so terrific for individual investors.

The one distinct advantage that callable preferred share issues have over non-callable preferred share issues is that, all things being equal, the callable issue will carry a higher yield. The problem is that you may not have the issue in your portfolio long enough to truly enjoy the greater yield because it could be close to being called. Here again, just as in bond investing, the best defence against call risk is to know what you own; be certain to ask about call provisions if you are being offered a preferred share with an exceptionally attractive yield.

Credit Risk

Preferred share issues are commonly referred to as "junior" debt. This means that the obligation to pay dividends to holders of a given preferred share rank after other creditors and bond holders. It's why investors need to set minimum quality criteria when shopping for preferred shares.

Some preferred share issues have a provision that enables the issuer to defer dividend payments in the event of financial hardship. A non-cumulative issue is one where the issuer can skip dividend payments in the event of financial disaster, resume at a later date and not have to make up missed payments. We prefer cumulative preferred shares (pun fully intended). Under a cumulative issue, the issuer will have to make up any missed payments. For an investor who is dependent upon a steady income stream from a portfolio, it is wise to focus on cumulative rather than non-cumulative issues.

Liquidity Risk

This form of risk deals with the relative ease with which an investor can dispose of an investment at or near fair-market value. For the buy-and-hold investor, this may not be much of a problem. For an investor who may need to remove money from the investment, though, liquidity risk can be quite significant. Will Rogers summed it up best when he said, "It's not return on my investment that I'm worried about—it's return *of* my investment."

One of the best methods we know of to check for the liquidity of a preferred share issue is to take a look at the spread between the bid and ask (offer) quotes. A preferred share offering with good liquidity will maintain a fairly narrow spread between the bid and ask quotes.

FINAL DOS AND DON'TS

The fixed-income or lending part of investing might best be summarized as securing required income while maintaining a vigilant lookout to take advantage of opportunities and defend against accompanying risks. It's a part of the process pivotal to overall investment success.

Diversify and guard against the associated risks and minimize the reinvestment risk through a laddered portfolio approach. Above all, don't succumb to the siren song of disproportionately high yields. The risk is seldom worth the reward.

Take basic steps like these and the fixed-income section of your portfolio could bring that extra degree of annual total return which compounded annually over a multi-year term makes that all-important difference in ultimate portfolio success.

Though very largely an ode to bonds, fixed-income investing is nonetheless the essential first part of a two-step process in which both steps must be approached in tandem. Now to the second step, that ultimate extension of term into those "perpetual bonds with floating rates of return" referred to earlier; namely, to investing in equities with which to build the real wealth that will be needed to ensure our investments last longer than we do.

CHAPTER 8

Building Blocks of Wealth

Equities

"Although falling stock prices will bring short term pain, this will ultimately benefit the long term investor who can buy and accumulate equities at the discounted prices. The fact that stock returns in the long run have surpassed other financial assets through market peaks and troughs attests to the resiliency of stocks in all economic and financial climates."

Jeremy J. Siegel, *Stocks for the Long Run*

PRIDE OF OWNERSHIP

Not too long ago, Michael sat enthralled as Hernando de Soto, the distinguished Peruvian economist and author of *The Mystery of Capital*, expounded on how the cycle of global poverty could be broken by allowing the poor to have proper legal title to their land and small businesses. "Own something, witnessed by a piece of paper you can take to a bank and borrow against. You'd be amazed how things get going!" The gist of an inspiring message was that ownership generates the creation of wealth, even at this humblest of levels. Equity investing from the ground up: that's what this indefatigable champion keeps on preaching as the key to a better world.

The examples of this approach in action are everywhere. Hong Kong billionaire Li Ka-shing began a rags-to-riches journey that saw him build Hutchison Whampoa into the world's largest independent port operator and acquire major stakes in Canadian corporate giants such as Canadian Imperial Bank of Commerce and Husky Energy. How did he start this vast business empire? With a small business making plastic flowers.

Closer to home, Roy Thomson, later Lord Thomson of Fleet, transformed a tiny radio station in Timmins, Ontario, into what was to become The Thomson Corporation, one of the world's leading information services providers. Frank Stronach (Magna International), Paul Desmarais (Power Corporation of Canada), and Mike Lazaridis and Jim Balsillie (Research in Motion) are other Canadian examples of what an entrepreneurial spirit and pride of ownership can ultimately become.

INVEST OR DIE

In February 1993, *Fortune* magazine ran a memorable cover story entitled "Invest or Die." In order to survive in an increasingly competitive world, corporations were urged to update plant, equipment and systems rather than merely cut costs.

There could be few better Canadian examples of this than another radio pioneer, Ted Rogers, who to this day continues to invest in his capital-intensive businesses through thick and thin. Without his non-stop urgency, Rogers Communications would not have grown into a world-ranking Canadian communications giant. There's a message in examples like these for all of us.

For most of us, with the possible exception of marrying well, winning the lottery or inheriting the estate of a wealthy relative, the only means of building true lasting wealth (whatever you may deem that to be) is through the ownership of enduring enterprises. We may not have the ability to turn plastic flowers into a global economic powerhouse, or tiny radio stations into a communications giant, but we can enjoy the benefits of business ownership through acquiring shares of top-flight companies. This way we will enjoy financial health and portfolio longevity that we wouldn't otherwise. Let equity ownership run, and watch how we prosper.

It's a challenge that takes on added meaning as life expectancies keep rising. Scotiabank ran an eye-catching advertisement in which someone comments to a friend that he is ready for retirement, but his RRSP isn't. To avoid a real-life predicament like this, we must ensure that the resources generating the income on which we are going to depend last longer than we do. There's really only one way: by building equity in portfolios customized to our age, time horizons and individual circumstances.

FIGHT OR FLIGHT

Unfortunately, many investors suffer their worst portfolio "injuries" with equities. The causes are many, with the most common detailed in chapters 2 and 3. You can't build that sought-after investment wealth without running risk. It's a four-letter word that must be properly understood, no matter how deeply we may or may not wish to involve ourselves in the investment process.

Adversity in the markets is almost without exception met by the most basic, instinctive human responses of fight or flight. Investors who choose to fight back can often fall prey to a casino syndrome and take on ever-growing degrees of risk in a bid to recoup lost capital. The invariable result is a compounding of the initial loss. At the other end of the response spectrum is the investor who flees the market in panic. Losses will be averted, but taking cover on the sidelines can prove to be very costly when taken over a span of years. Think back to the first chapter when we recalled the time in the early 1980s when equities were so terribly out of favour with the investing public. With the benefit of hindsight we can now see how costly short-term thinking was to investors of that period.

Risk is acceptable, provided it can be diversified and hedged against. Building wealth through the use of stock ownership without subjecting oneself to catastrophic losses is the real test. To repeat our earlier baseball analogy, you should be consistently trying to get runners on base. Swinging for the fences with every at-bat only serves to increase your number of strikeouts.

THE EIGHTH WONDER

Home ownership is one form of equity investment everyone can understand. Borrow in the form of a mortgage to buy a home that grows in value and the resulting differential is equity that belongs to you, the owner. In the process, it can also serve a number of useful purposes.

In recent years American homeowners have repeatedly refinanced their homes to take advantage of historically low borrowing costs and mortgage rates. However, instead of investing the capital raised from these refinancing bonanzas, they have continued to spend excessively, regardless of middling economic circumstances and a questionable employment market. This cavalier approach escalates the reverse risk when interest rates rise, property values fall and home equity turns negative. Then, you'll owe the mortgage lender the difference, rather than they you—an experience that legions of homeowners in Alberta and Britain can still painfully testify to.

Nevertheless, few would argue against the wealth-building power of this most understandable and worthwhile form of equity ownership. Even after the devastating real estate crashes of the 1980s in Alberta and the 1990s in Britain, shrewd investors capitalized on properties listed at "fire sale" prices to amass great wealth as these markets recovered and prices rose. The goal in stock market investing is much the same: to find reasonably priced or, better yet, fundamentally undervalued shares in which to invest. This way, time can work the magic of compounding, once described by Albert Einstein as "the eighth wonder of the world."

RISK VS. REWARD

In corporations, the shareholders' equity is what remains for the true owners, the common shareholders, after all other claims on their assets have been satisfied. Likewise, common shareholder earnings are the residue after all annual costs have been met, including contractual payments such as interest on outstanding debt. The resultant "bottom-line" earnings can then be disbursed in whole or part as dividends, or added to shareholders' equity for reinvestment in the business. Of course, the opposite happens if a company is unsuccessful; then, bottom-line losses are subtracted from shareholders' equity, which is depleted as a result. Either way, the success or failure of an equity investment becomes recognized in rising or falling share prices in the stock marketplace.

Shareholder earnings are, by definition, dependent upon variables such as sales, material costs, write-offs, interest on debt and taxes. It follows that management's capabilities must be a major consideration when evaluating a company's stock. The often-delicate balance between risk and reward that management must wrestle with is also the ongoing challenge faced by every investor. Equal parts of patience and cool logic to achieve the optimal balance between risk and reward are necessary ingredients at the individual investor level as well.

Do Your Homework!

Michael long remembers his investments in fledgling International Thomson Organisation and in the leftover rag-tags of bankrupted Royal Trustco that had been assembled in a new company called Gentra. In due course, International Thomson was transformed into Thomson Corporation and Gentra into Brookfield Properties. Both are now among Michael's largest and most successful investments. The moral of the story: do your homework. Identify true bargains and be prepared to stick with them when the facts justify your patience.

When everything is working smoothly, little else can compare to the wealth-building power of growing companies. Michael fondly recalls the five shares of Canadian Pacific Railway he bought for his now-adult daughter at her birth. Dividends were automatically reinvested through the company's dividend reinvestment plan, and by the time young Julia Graham was ready to enter university, much of her tuition could be covered by that initial investment of a few hundred dollars.

TYPES OF RISK FACTORS

"That which does not kill us makes us stronger." This famous quote from Frederic Nietzsche could easily be adopted for use and attested to by hard-bitten equity investors. Even at the best of times, equity investing can also be a humbling experience. Your authors can ruefully testify to costly forays in Air Canada (now ACE Aviation Holdings), Bombardier, Nortel Networks, Massey-Ferguson, Royal Trustco, Saskatchewan Wheat Pool and others. Investing in the stock market must, by definition, include accompanying scrapes and bruises. To ensure that the damage isn't terminal, it's important to have a clear understanding of how much risk you are exposed to, and can realistically run.

Understand that if you're going invest in the stock market, either directly through ownership of shares or indirectly through third-party money managers (mutual funds, wrap accounts, etc.), there is no such thing as a free lunch. Because risk will always be present in some form, an understanding of the various types of risk will help you identify problems sooner and take action before a situation progresses from difficult to dire.

There are two basic types of risk from which others will flow. Let's begin our quick tour of the wonderful world of risk with the two main varieties: systemic risk and unsystemic risk. We'll explore risk and risk management strategies in greater detail in the next chapter after getting started with the fundamentals.

Systemic Risk

Systemic risk influences a wide range of assets, and is virtually impossible to insulate oneself against. It's a type of risk sometimes referred to as "event risk." Think back, for example, to the 1995 Quebec referendum on sovereignty. Had the separatists carried the day, there would almost certainly have been some major near-term dislocation of the Canadian capital markets. Another example of systemic or event risk is the major decline of the mighty U.S. dollar that has taken place in the world's foreign exchange markets. It's a subject we'll return to when discussing related risks—in this case, foreign exchange.

Unsystemic Risk

Unsystemic risk refers to the kind of risk that is more narrowly focused: The most common example would be a negative earnings report from a company. The bad news affects the value of the shares in question and could possibly also have an adverse influence upon share prices of other companies in the same sector. It's this type of risk that is best guarded against through proper portfolio diversification, another discussion for later in this chapter.

Now that we've introduced you to "the big two," let's get acquainted with some of the other forms of risk you're likely to encounter.

Foreign Exchange Risk

From a geographic perspective, Canada is one big country. Comparatively, however, our capital markets are quite diminutive. As a result, many Canadian investors wisely choose to add a layer of additional diversification to their portfolios by including securities from beyond Canada's borders.

In retrospect, the raising in 2000 of the foreign content limit in RRSPs to 30% from 20% couldn't have come at a worse time. Why? Because a frequently overlooked risk attached to this type of diversification relates to foreign exchange. Through 2003 and 2004, many Canadian investors with expanded U.S. dollar-denominated assets were adversely impacted by the Canadian dollar's steep rise in value against the U.S. dollar. As a result, the performance of the U.S. equity section of their portfolios, in what were good years in the U.S. stock markets, was heavily negated when converted back to Canadian dollars. Now that the 2005 Federal budget has removed the 30% foreign content limit, there is a level playing field for all. With institutions and individual investors now able to invest worldwide, Canadian corporations will never be as sheltered as they once were. We see this as a distinct advantage for Canadian investors and for companies that can meet the challenge of greater competition for investor capital.

Interest-Rate Risk

Rising interest rates are another risk that can be particularly detrimental to the shares of interest-sensitive securities such as bonds, banks, pipelines, utilities and income trusts, in other words, to securities that are known for their yields. Thus, a secure yield on a pipeline stock will be perceived as more valuable by investors in a falling as opposed to a rising interest-rate environment. The stock markets can usually live with interest rates at any level, but become very unsettled when rates begin rising and they must run interest rate risk.

Market Risk

Beta—not in reference to the type of video in use before much of the world went to VHS for their video collections—reflects market risk synonymous with volatility. Beta is simply a tool to help investors understand how much risk they are likely assuming with a given security. It's the degree of a given stock's volatility versus the overall market that can be tracked and measured over time. A high beta stock is one that has historically demonstrated greater swings in value than the appropriate market index. Growth stocks typically have a higher beta than interest-sensitive stocks. Beta can also be used to measure the degree of price volatility on a mutual fund versus a benchmark index such as the S&P 500.

Regardless of the types and levels of risk, all stocks must still run a gauntlet, the corollary of which is reward. Risk and reward are connected at the hip. You can't have the one without the other, but in order to enjoy more of the rewards, first cover off the risks to the greatest degree possible.

THE PRICE MUST BE RIGHT

Warren Buffett likes to answer "forever" when asked how long he holds stocks. We stated in an earlier chapter that a good rule is to take your losses quickly and your profits slowly. The reluctance to sell stocks on which dividends are paid and the price continuously appreciates is understandable, but even Mr. Buffett will admit that nothing is forever. Eventually there will come a time when circumstances change or better values emerge elsewhere, or when the wisest course of action is to trim back holdings that have become disproportionately large within a portfolio, or when holdings become sufficiently overpriced to warrant switching into investments judged to offer better value. Investing always involves a shifting sea of values in which everything is relative; to be successful, investors must be prepared to make appropriate adjustments in this knowledge.

In art, what customers are prepared to pay lies in the eye of the beholder. In investing, the price you are prepared to pay, or the value you place on shares of a company, can be similarly subjective. You invest in a company anticipating it will generate a stream of future earnings. That seems to be a reasonable proposition, but to get a proper fix on the worth of the investment you must estimate these earnings annually and discount them back to the present at what you consider a suitable interest rate. If the resultant present value is higher than today's share price, it's an investment offering value. If the present value is much higher, you could have unearthed an investment bargain. If the present value is lower, you would be wise to invest your hard-earned dollars elsewhere.

VALUE INVESTING AND ITS HEART AND SOUL: THE P/E RATIO

One such alternative is bonds, on which, subject to credit worthiness (another risk), the regular interest payment and the repayment of principal are exactly known. This is why bond yields are frequently used as benchmarks in equity valuation exercises. In turn, this leads to the price-to-earnings ratio, or P/E, on the stock you are considering. Invert this ratio to determine earnings-to-price, in other words, the yield in earnings terms, and see how it compares with yields on longer-term bonds. Generally, the higher the P/E, the lower the earnings yield and the less favourable the comparison, unless earnings are estimated to grow so strongly that when they are discounted to the present, a high P/E is justified. More on that shortly.

Optional refinements round out this basic valuation exercise. It is useful to determine the P/E ratio of a company and then compare it against the P/Es of companies in the same industry to get a sense of how (from a valuation perspective, at least) the company holds up against its rivals. If, however, the company in question is a resource company extracting difficult-to-measure assets in the ground, you'll probably be better off judging the future cash flows rather than earnings.

EBITDA, an acronym for earnings before interest, taxes, depreciation and amortization, is another measure that is used by research analysts and investment professionals. Actual cash earnings before interest expenses, amortization and taxes is certainly more tangible than bottom-line earnings and is a criterion many investment managers prefer, regardless. Still more criteria are the underlying physical assets translated into book value per share, or what these assets might be worth in market terms. It's an exercise that can be broadened to include liquid (i.e., cash and near-cash) assets on hand, and working capital represented by current assets less current liabilities.

Benjamin Graham used to determinedly search for stocks below their book value or, even better, below their working capital per share. For investors requiring income while they wait for stocks to reach their true value, the search should consider a company's ability to pay dividends to its shareholders. We particularly like companies where there is a history of dividend increases over a span of many years—more on this later.

THE WORLD ACCORDING TO GARP

A close relative to value investing is the GARP style of security selection—growth at a reasonable price. Whereas a value investor will hunt for companies that, in the words of Warren Buffett, offer a "margin of safety," a GARP investor is willing to take on incrementally greater risk in the search for profit. An investor employing the GARP method of stock selection is on the prowl for companies that demonstrate the potential to grow their earnings at a pace faster than their peer group. In this respect, GARP investors are not much different from growth investors, except that they set strict limits on how much they are prepared to pay for the potential earnings growth, usually using the price-to-earnings ratio as their yardstick. Like Warren Buffett, the GARP investor is looking for some margin of safety, just maybe not quite so much as their value compatriot.

GROWTH AND MOMENTUM INVESTING

We've put these two styles of stock selection together because they are so often synonymous, but they aren't truly identical. As alluded to a moment ago, a growth investor is an investor seeking companies that are capable of delivering an above-average rate of growth in their sales and earnings. A biotech company with an exciting new development to treat disease would be a typical example. Growth investors may not be completely unconcerned about valuation metrics, but they are far less conscious of them than GARP and value investors.

Momentum investing occurs when an investor is looking for direction from the analyst community to uncover candidates for investment (we're talking stock analysts here, but at times psychoanalytic assistance wouldn't be such a bad thing, either!). The momentum investor combs through reams of analyst reports looking for an emerging consensus to raise investment ratings, price objectives or target prices. If the classic formula for profitable investing is to buy low and sell high, the momentum investor alters the formula to read buy high and sell higher. Momentum investors are most often the least concerned about valuation.

KNOW WHAT YOU OWN

In Chapter 3 we described how the mood at the 2000 annual general meeting of shareholders of Berkshire Hathaway Inc., the corporate home of the legendary Warren Buffett, was not quite as usual. The major market averages, and the technology-driven NASDAQ Composite Index in particular, had turned in eye-popping returns for the year gone by, but the shares of Berkshire, while profitable for investors, were unremarkable by comparison. The reason was a complete absence of technology holdings in the Berkshire stable of companies because Buffett and Munger did not have the thorough understanding of these businesses that they customarily require. In their lexicon, failure to understand how a business operates, and, more importantly how it generates profits for investors was, and is, tantamount to speculation. How could investors possibly make a rational decision to buy or sell shares of a company if they didn't have the requisite understanding of what they were investing in? Neither felt that they had a sufficient grasp of the various forms of new technology or the companies delivering it to make sound investment decisions. It was a conviction to be vindicated subsequently by the bursting of the tech bubble.

You needn't be a geologist to invest in a mining company, but you should know that Company X mines copper and what the outlook for copper is before you make an investment in the company's shares. Anything less, as Warren Buffett might say, is pure speculation.

SURF AND TURF

The mismatching of stocks with investor needs is a sure path to pain and disappointment. Someone with a deadly shellfish allergy wouldn't be foolish enough to order surf and turf in a restaurant, yet it's alarming how many times investors unwittingly commit a comparable act. Instead, portfolios should contain only securities that match investors' tolerance for risk. Thus, a conservatively ranked investor should not be in speculative mining stocks; or an investor who can afford to run higher risks excessively in utility stocks.

For this reason, we urge investors, regardless of whether they prefer active or passive management of their precious capital, to at least have some working knowledge of how their investments function. This also means you should never be shy about bringing in outside help when you, and possibly your advisor, don't have the requisite skills.

Highly specialized market segments such as biotechnology, or little known geographic regions such as the emerging markets, are classic examples of this need. As professionals who earn their living from proffering investment advice, we are the first to admit that investing is far too humbling an experience not to seek access to expert counsel, and we especially welcome questions from investors in the setting-up stage.

INVESTOR, KNOW THYSELF

Which equities are right for you in going about the challenge of how best to assemble those necessary blocks of wealth? The answers can require soul searching, as well as consideration given to:

- your time horizon
- the financial resources at your disposal
- your need for income now versus capital appreciation later
- your tax bracket
- the commitment of time and energy you are prepared to give your investments
- how much you can afford to risk

A 20% annual gain on an investment is an enticing achievement few investors would ignore. Turn it around, though, and ask yourself how you might cope with a 20% loss. Behavioural finance is a veritable industry devoted to answering such questions. "What's *your* number?" is an all-embracing question we will return to in Chapter 12, but we will note that in coming up with the answer to this overriding question, it's once again all about you.

SPREAD THE WEALTH—BUT NOT TOO THIN

The risk-busting rule of diversification is critical in building the equity component of portfolios to include the right blend of different stocks in different industries. If you were to poll a sampling of Canadian investment managers you would find that each has his or her own ceiling beyond which a portfolio can become unwieldy.

Dr. Graham's Prescription

Drawing on his four decades of slogging it out in the trenches of Bay Street, Michael has developed a stock-picking pattern that has served him well. He begins with the basics: searching out industries where the conditions are judged to be favourable.

He then moves in closer to examine the earnings record of a company that may have caught his eye in a favoured sector. In so doing, he places particular importance on the previous five years' worth of earnings to help identify any trends.

Next, he focuses on industry analysts' estimates of that company's current and future-year earnings per share. From these he can assess and compare the price-to-earnings ratios based on trailing and forward earnings (i.e., latest 12-month reported earnings and estimated future earnings), and work through the valuation procedure described previously. He particularly notes the payout record, the dividend currently indicated and the dividend yield.

Finally, Michael looks at the 52-week price record to get an idea of how the shares are favoured in today's marketplace. Out of a monitoring process like this comes a blue-chip "shopping" list, as illustrated in the table. It's a list in which stocks worthy of consideration are grouped by sector—beginning with the natural resources for which Canada is famous, followed by downstream industrials and manufacturers, then switching to the consumer sector and all that relates (including real estate and diversified management holding companies), and concluding with financial services such as banks, insurers and wealth managers.

Others, including the Toronto Stock Exchange set up their groupings and their sub-indexes differently. The Toronto Stock Exchange is in the process of adding a 14th sub-index for income trusts to its benchmark S&P/TSX Composite Index. The point of the exercise is to set up a system whereby you and/or your advisor can keep on top of constantly changing prices and relative values.

Remember, too, that not every name on a shopping list like this will make it into every portfolio. Whereas an existing client may hold a stock that was once favoured for purchase, a newer client may not because the stock has risen to a level where it is no longer judged to be a bargain. Just as it is always a good idea to go grocery shopping with a list in hand to ward off unfortunate or impulsive purchases, so it is advisable to enter the investment markets with a shopping list clenched firmly in hand.

Even a perfunctory study of the accompanying table reveals the range of variables to be contended with. Earnings growth is never assured and earnings can fluctuate widely in the resource and cyclical sectors in particular. Price-earnings ratios can also range widely, depending on the expected degree of growth and associated risk. (Thus, growth stocks traditionally have higher P/E ratios than cyclicals.) Dividends and dividend yields can vary too, depending on the corporate need for profits to be reinvested in further growth. Many international companies report their earnings—and sometimes pay their dividends—in U.S. dollars, this practice requiring adjustment for currency conversion and risk.

In Chapter 2, we recommended an optimum number of holdings in the equity section of most portfolios. A continuously fresh shopping list of about 25 names facilitates this optimum selection process.

6-PAKS

From his selection lists Michael has also developed his own distinctive 6-Paks of Canadian stocks, which, bought as packages, have worked out very well. His recommended Canadian 6-Pak for 2004 is shown on page 129. Over a challenging year it appreciated by an above-average 25% and yielded 2% on the dividends received, for a total return of 27%. An essential requisite is to purchase the six in a more or less equal range in dollar terms (between $3,000 and $4,000, in this example). Six is probably too small a number for diversification purposes, but nonetheless makes up a useful and affordable package for purchase in multi-pak form. Not all six stocks always go up; this particular 6-Pak included one significant loser (Thomson Corporation). Neither do these 6-Paks always work out as successfully as in 2004, but go about a package approach properly, stay with class and quality, and it's amazing how successfully the years will add up—and the equity wealth will build.

BLUE CHIP CANADIAN EQUITY "SHOPPING" LIST – SUMMER 2005

Stock	Stock[1] Symbol	Price Jun 30	2000	Earnings Per Share[2] 2003	2004	2005E	Price-Est. Earn	Indicat. Divid.[3]	Curr. Yield	52-Week High	Low
EnCana Corporation	ECA	$48.83	n/a	4.65[+4]	5.32[+4]	6.15[+4]	6.5[4]	0.37	0.7%	$51.27	$26.15
Husky Energy	HSE	48.73	1.39	3.25	2.36	2.60	18.7	0.56	1.1	50.75	25.42
Suncor Energy	SU	57.92	2.05[4]	4.93[4]	4.86[4]	6.00[4]	9.7[4]	0.24	0.4	60.24	32.80
Enbridge	ENB	34.95	2.32	4.03	3.86	4.20	8.3	1.00	2.9	36.19	23.62
TransCanada Corp.	TRP	32.24	1.50	1.66	1.58	1.75	18.4	1.22	3.8	33.03	25.37
Alcan	AL	36.78	2.75[+]	1.67[+]	2.15[+]	2.60[+]	11.5	0.60[+]	2.0	56.08	36.56
Barrick Gold Corp.	ABX	30.60	-2.22[+]	0.37[+]	0.46[+]	0.80[+]	31.2	0.22[+]	0.9	31.80	24.10
Inco	N	46.15	1.97[+]	0.66[+]	2.99[+]	3.30[+]	11.4	0.40[+]	1.1	53.84	39.32
Teck Cominco	TEK.SV.B	41.34	0.66	0.49	3.45	4.10	10.1	0.80	1.9	48.00	22.36
Abitibi-Consolidated	A	5.46	0.94	-0.85	-0.35	0.00	n/a	0.10	1.8	9.28	4.92
Canadian Pacific Railway	CP	42.39	2.54	2.07	2.27	3.25	13.0	0.60	1.4	46.88	31.60
Dofasco	DFS	38.60	2.45	1.55	4.77	3.90	9.9	1.32	3.4	46.37	31.25
Magna International	MG.SV.A	86.06	6.46[+]	5.19[+]	7.13[+]	7.50[+]	9.4	1.87	2.2	114.00	75.00
Canadian Tire	CTR.NV	56.62	1.89	2.81	3.30	3.80	14.9	0.58	1.0	62.24	43.66
George Weston	WN	108.32	3.70	5.91	4.49	6.00	18.0	1.44	1.3	115.51	86.25
BCE Inc.	BCE	29.00	0.62	2.09	2.00	2.20	13.2	1.32	4.6	30.46	25.72
Telus Corporation	T	41.79	1.85	0.92	1.58	2.00	20.9	0.80	1.9	43.38	19.21
Thomson Corporation	TOC	41.02	1.96[+]	1.34[+]	1.54[+]	1.75[+]	19.1	0.80[+]	2.4	45.89	38.80
Brookfield Properties	BPO	34.65	0.63[+]	1.08[+]	0.71[+]	1.30[+]	22.2	0.72[+]	2.5	35.80	25.03
Brascan Corporation	BNN.LV.A	46.80	1.53	1.31	2.38	2.80	16.7	0.74	1.6	48.76	34.60
Power Corp. of Canada	POW	30.72	1.25	1.76	2.08	2.40	12.8	0.68	2.2	32.75	25.93
Bank of Nova Scotia	BNS	40.54	1.81	2.34	2.82	3.30	12.2	1.36	3.4	41.72	34.91
Manulife Financial	MFC	58.51	2.22	3.31	3.62	4.25	13.8	1.20	2.1	60.70	50.50
Royal Bank of Canada	RY	75.90	3.40	4.42	4.25	5.75	13.2	2.44	3.2	77.25	56.61
Toronto Dominion Bank	TD	54.64	1.56	1.51	3.39	4.15	13.2	1.60	2.9	56.20	42.54

Sources: Company annual reports, investment dealer research reports, Bloomberg
Notes: E – Estimated; taken:from Canadian investment industry research; + Reported/paid in U.S. dollars; 1. Symbol on Toronto Stock Exchange; 2. Fully diluted and before unusual items (as best possible to ascertain); 3. Indicated annual rate based on latest quarterly (or interim) declaration; 4. Cash Flow (rather than earnings)

Canadian 6-Pak—2004 Model

	No. of Shares	Share Price Jan. 1	Share Price Dec. 31	Market Value Jan. 1	Market Value Dec. 31	Year-End Dividend [1]
Canadian Pacific Railway	100	36.58	41.10	3,658	4,110	53
EnCana Corporation	60	51.00	68.70	3,060	4,122	29
Manulife Financial	75	41.85	55.40	3,139	4,155	78
Teck Cominco	150	21.93	36.92	3,290	5,538	60
Thomson Corporation	75	47.08	42.27	3,531	3,170	69 [2]
Toronto-Dominion Bank	80	43.29	49.92	3,463	3,994	115
				$20,141	$25,089	$404

(1) Annual level indicated by latest quarterly payment.
(2) Payable in U.S. dollars converted to Canadian.

QUINTESSENTIAL DIVIDENDS

At the height of the tech stock boom of the late 1990s, Michael saved a cartoon from some forgotten business publication as a reminder of just how distorted prevailing market "wisdom" could become. In it, three young employees are gathered in the presence of a senior executive. The juniors ask in astonishment, *"And these dividends they used to hand out—where exactly did the money come from?"* That one cartoon spoke volumes for the ethos of the day.

Despite the twisted logic of the boom times, and throughout the savage bear market that was to follow, dividends remain what they've always been—cash disbursements born out of a company's earnings. What has changed is their ever-growing role both for tax and investment reasons and the underlying support their payment can provide.

In the United States, the Bush administration's tax reforms have included cutting the taxes payable on dividends to a maximum of 15% (from as high as 35%). Could there be a link with the fact that in 2004, more than half of the companies making up the S&P 500 Index either raised their dividend payouts or implemented dividend policies for the first time? Such is the growing popularity of dividends that even high-growth companies like Microsoft are now paying them quarterly.

In Canada, where dividend tax credits were implemented many years before, the effective tax on dividends is now higher than in the United States. Nevertheless, tax rates on dividends of 24% to 37% (depending on the province) compare with top income-tax brackets of between 44% and 48%. Thus the incentive remains in Canada to boost after-tax income through dividends.

In addition, there is a growing realization of what powerful longer-term stimulants dividends can come to represent. An absorbing *New York Times* article entitled "Does Your Portfolio Need a Dividend Kick?" (November 14, 2004) illustrated how stocks in the S&P 500 Index that pay regular dividends generally outperform those that do not.

Best of all is to find companies with leading industry positions, financial strength and exemplary earnings and dividend records. It's not so much the initial yield but dividends and yields growing over time that make stocks like these such valuable investments. Compare current dividend levels with the per share payments to shareholders, say five or 10 years ago, and you'll be astounded at how the yield has risen on the original cost.

Michael has also broadened his Canadian 6-Paks to include dividends. Here, too, it's an approach built on more or less equal dollar investments in half a dozen top-flight, financially strong, world-class Canadian corporations expected to raise their dividend payments to shareholders annually—an ironclad requirement for inclusion. His Canadian Dividend 6-Pak for 2004 is shown below. An annual return of 26%, of which 24% was represented by capital appreciation, was not only exceptional but lucky. It nonetheless illustrates how a focus on rising, built-in dividends can also bring the bonus of superior total returns.

Canadian Dividend 6-Pak—2004 Model

	No. of Shares	Share Price Jan. 1	Share Price Dec. 31	Market Value Jan. 1	Market Value Dec. 31	Indic. Dividend[1] Jan. 1	Indic. Dividend[1] Dec. 31
Bank of Nova Scotia [2]	100	22.90	40.70	3,290	4,070	100	128
Brascan Corporation. [2]	112[3]	26.82	43.15	3,004	4,833	92	92
Manulife Financial	75	41.85	55.40	3,139	4,155	59	73
Power Corp. of Canada	150[3]	24.20	31.00	3,630	4,650	73	60
Toronto-Dominion Bank[2]	75	43.29	49.92	3,247	3,744	102	115
Thomson Corpration[2]	75	47.08	42.27	3,531	3,170	74[3]	68[3]
				$19,841	$24,622	$500	$549

Notes:
(1)   Annual level indicated by latest quarterly payment.
(2)   Offer dividend re-investment plan.
(3)   Adjusted for subsequent stock splits.
(4)   Payable in U.S. dollars converted to Canadian dollars.

When you invest in well-managed companies that regularly raise their dividends to their shareholders, you experience the equivalent to compounding.

Reinvest these dividends in more shares of the same company and it becomes double compounding, in which Albert Einstein's "eighth wonder" effect on individual net worth will happen even faster. Note how four holdings in the Canadian Dividend 6-Pak also offer dividend reinvestment plans (DRIPs).

In his newest book, *The Future for Investors: Why the Tried and the True Triumph Over the Bold and the New*, Jeremy Siegel contends that steady dividends and reasonable valuations always trump growth. We couldn't agree more.

MUTUAL FUNDS

"Yes, I accept the need for building blocks of wealth called equities. But for all sorts of valid reasons—earning my livelihood, my hobbies, my commitment to raising a family and a lack of inclination—I would prefer others handle my investing for me." Statements like these are entirely logical. This is where mutual funds enter the picture. They offer the same long-term strategic focus, the same golden rules of balance and diversification and ultimately the same end goal as investments selected directly by investors. There are some important differences of approach, though, that you will need to understand.

Instead of shares and 6-Paks, there will be units in managed funds of your choice. You'll still own shares through which to build that necessary wealth, but indirectly rather than directly. You'll be a passive rather than an active investor, with others doing the stockpicking for you. There's absolutely nothing wrong with this approach, only a need to go about it properly.

Mutual funds are also often used to good effect for representation in sectors where the investor and advisor have clear limitations. A frequent example is a need to understand foreign markets and accounting for international diversification. Often, it is more efficient to gain international diversification through a global or country mutual fund in which others have the "on-the-ground" experience and expertise you and your advisor may lack. The same applies in fast-growing, higher-risk sectors like technology and health care. Never hesitate to bring in outside experts where appropriate; failed investing is just too humbling to refuse outside assistance. Take note, however, that the market for mutual funds is a crowded field that needs to be entered with care. Hence, you must choose your mutual funds with as much deliberation as you would take in selecting individual stocks.

The pioneering days when the Canadian mutual fund universe consisted of the Canadian Investment Fund and not much else are long gone. Today, there are more mutual funds in Canada and the U.S. than there are stocks listed on the Toronto and New York stock exchanges. Just open the financial pages in any daily newspaper to see what we mean. How fortunate to have such a complete range: asset allocation, balanced, diversified, growth equity, high yield, income and growth, sector, international and more. At the same time, there are some important considerations to be made before dropping your precious savings into the lap of a mutual fund manager.

1. Always inquire about the track record of the mutual funds your advisor is recommending for you. How have they done over the past one, three and five years? How do their records stack up against other funds in the same sectors, as well as against established benchmarks like the S&P 500 and TSX 300 indexes? Try, where possible, to stay with funds and fund managers who have remained in the first or second quartile relative to their peer group over extended periods of time. We recommend five years as a minimum time (see below for a definition of quartile rankings).

2. Fees charged by mutual fund companies to manage unit holder capital are a source of steady criticism in today's business press. We are always more than willing to pay a premium for performance; however, management expense ratios (MERs) that range between 2% and 3% of total fund assets can be all the more expensive if the fund doesn't perform as expected. An indifferent performance record and a relatively high MER could be the warning flags to steer you away from disappointment.

3. Pay attention to the manager of the fund you are considering, and the length of time he or she has been at the helm. If the fund in question has a terrific five-year track record, but the present-day manager has been there for only five months, the past performance needs to be deeply discounted or maybe thrown out all together.

Quartile Rankings

A mutual fund's quartile ranking is a measure of how its performance stacks up against similarly mandated funds over a specific time frame. A first-quartile ranking, for example, means that the fund's performance put it in the top 25% of all funds in its category. Having a second-quartile ranking is still good, but not as impressive as a first-quartile ranking. Some fund managers will nonetheless consciously try to deliver second-quartile performance on a regular basis. This could be because the fund the manager is responsible for has been designed with conservative investors in mind and an attempt at a first-quartile ranking may expose investors to higher levels of risk than would otherwise have been the case. While this is plausible, no manager can make the claim of *trying* to achieve third- or fourth-quartile performance. Funds with such performance are usually best avoided.

PASSIVE VS. ACTIVE MANAGEMENT

The debate among investment professionals on the merits of active or passive management rages with an intensity reminiscent of the Hatfields and McCoys.

Passive asset management is achieved through the use of hybrid investment vehicles like index funds and exchange traded funds. Active asset management occurs when the services of a third party manager enter the picture. This manager takes on the responsibility for selecting, buying and selling securities in accordance with a pre-defined mandate. Under passive management, there is no fund manager making day-to-day security selection decisions. Instead, investment "decisions" involve the tracking or mimicking of a benchmark index such as the S&P 500, or a sub-index such as the TSX 300 financial services sub-index. With no manager to pay, and a low turnover of stocks, passive management fund vehicles often offer the attribute of rock-bottom pricing. It's a little like a do-it-yourself home repair rather than having a contractor coming into your home to do the job for you.

Critics of passive management cite the inability to deliver returns superior to the major market averages on the upside but the ability to deliver returns every bit as painful as the market averages on the downside as their reasons for avoiding this approach. Similarly, critics of active management point to the very small band of asset managers who are consistently able to beat the market and the higher attendant costs as reasons why they refuse to hire an asset manager.

CORE AND EXPLORE: THE THIRD WAY

Much has been said over the years of British Prime Minister Tony Blair's "third way," a political middle ground between liberalism and conservatism. A "third way" has also emerged in the epic struggle between active and passive investment management. It has grown in popularity with the widespread acceptance of exchange traded funds (ETFs). An exchange traded fund is, as the name implies, a fund that is actively traded on the stock markets. These funds typically offer the investor a passive approach to investing in either an entire stock market index, or one of the many sub-indexes. Barclays Global Investors, arguably the most prolific creator and marketer of ETFs, has spent considerable time and energy promoting its third way, dubbed the "core and explore" strategy.

Core and explore enables an investor to enjoy the cost savings and transparency that exchange traded funds can offer, together with the proactive assertiveness of active management.

This type of management differs from traditional active management in that the investor uses passive management tools to actively manage his or her portfolio. An investor utilizing core and explore as his or her preferred strategy would start by building a core, or foundation, of passive index-related investments to achieve a high level of diversification and cost efficiency. Once the core has been established, the investor would then move to spicing things up a little by adding more narrowly focused investments into the portfolio. This could be anything from individual stocks to mutual funds, closed-end funds or hedge funds. The core and explore investor takes a buy-and-hold approach to the core, while actively adjusting the assets outside of the core—the explore component—for maximum gain.

IN THE LONG RUN

In his epic work, *The Intelligent Investor*, Benjamin Graham wrote that "investing is most intelligent when it is most businesslike." His renowned disciple, Warren Buffett singles these words out as *the* nine most important words in all of investing. Jeremy Siegel, whom we quoted at the start of this chapter, explains that while investing is never easy, the longer-term returns on equities have surpassed those on all other financial assets. There you have the link between the two; go about investing in a business-like fashion and focus this approach on wealth-building equities in the knowledge that they bring superior, long-term returns. Whether you do so actively or passively, invest in an intelligent, business-like fashion, and be confident of the superior returns that are bound to follow.

In Canada, comparative statistics don't go back nearly as far as in the U.S., but they tell a similar story. The first of the accompanying charts compares the cumulative returns from the various beginning years (going back as far as 1956) to the end of the year 2000. It illustrates what a dollar invested in a sampling of Canadian stocks bonds or cash would have grown to from the beginning of the year in which the investment was made to the end of 2000. In so doing, it clearly illustrates how the longer the investment is held, the greater the emerging advantage of equities over bonds or cash. The second chart illustrates how even greater the equity advantage becomes if dividends are reinvested annually and compounding is allowed to work its magic.

The bear market setbacks of 2001 and 2002 mean that today's equity numbers would be only modestly higher. Also that their cumulative advantage over bonds has narrowed somewhat (the benefits of balance and diversification). Nevertheless the overall principle still applies; the longer that equities are held, the greater their relative superiority to fixed-income investments in delivering long-term growth. Remember, these charts are of averages. Now think what the added advantage of investing—and reinvesting—in *above-average* equity products could come to mean.

REMEMBER INFLATION?

Just in case you need a little more convincing that carefully selected shares of great, enduring companies need to have a place in your portfolio, stop to consider the erosionary effects of inflation. Mercifully, the double-digit inflation of the late 1970s and early 1980s is now but a distant memory. Even so, inflation remains a fact of life, even at today's greatly diminished levels.

The most vulnerable to its long-term effects are those on a fixed income, typically retirees. Look again at the charts we've included for you. No other asset class offers a better hedge against the long-term ravages of inflation than equities. Though you may be investing primarily for income rather than growth, having even a small component of your portfolio devoted to growth/equity investing will help to ensure that your assets will be as valuable to you 20 years from now as they are today.

Equities Build Long-Term Wealth Best
Value of $1 Invested in Canadian Securities*

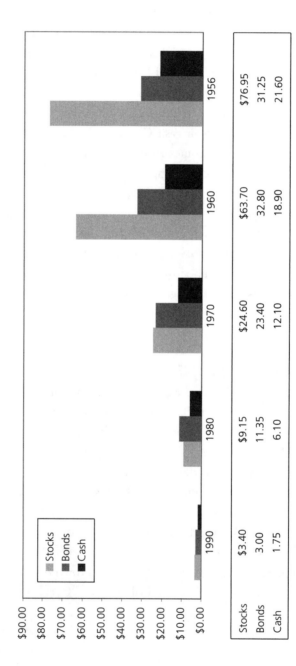

	Stocks	Bonds	Cash
1956	$76.95	31.25	21.60
1960	$63.70	32.80	18.90
1970	$24.60	23.40	12.10
1980	$9.15	11.35	6.10
1990	$3.40	3.00	1.75

*From the year shown to end 2000

Value of $1000 Invested in the TSE 300
– January 1956 To December 1999*

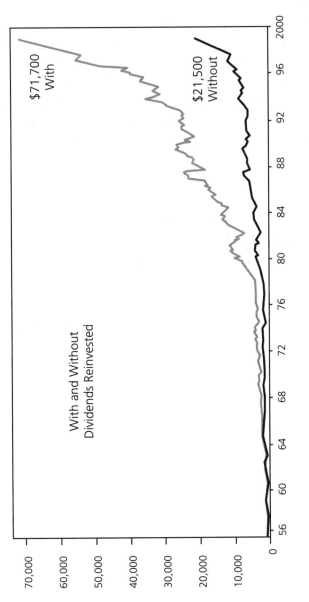

With and Without
Dividends Reinvested

$71,700
With

$21,500
Without

* Without BCE and Nortel, the growth with dividends reinvested would have been to $59,700.

BUILT TO LAST

The title to this chapter, "Building Blocks of Wealth: Equities," is intentionally ambiguous. Do we go about building blocks of wealth using equities, or are equities building blocks of wealth that must be in portfolios to ensure longer-term well-being? Either way the answer is an emphatic *yes*.

The ownership of great, enduring enterprises is made possible through share ownership, and it is these shares that serve as the building blocks for a portfolio that can stand the test of time. Just as you would never build a home with strictly one type of building material, we strongly encourage most investors, even self-described conservative investors, to include some degree of share ownership in their portfolios. This can be done by owning shares of companies directly, or indirectly through the use of mutual funds, exchange traded funds and so on. How you tap into the tremendous wealth-building potential of share ownership is up to you.

Your aim may not be to build a family fortune to rival that of the DuPonts' or the Rothschilds', yet the inescapable fact is that we are all living longer, more active lives than the generations that preceded us. The danger for many of today's investors is not that they will lose their money: it is that they will outlive it. It is for this reason that owning a piece of the corporations that are the foundation of our economy is imperative. Constructing a portfolio to meet long-range objectives absent of equities is akin to making a house constructed of cardboard. Use the proper materials in a prudent and professional manner, and your portfolio will last to meet your financial needs today, and for the many years to come.

CHAPTER 9

Running With Scissors
Prescriptions for Managing Risk

Risk is common to all forms of investing, yet a critical but often overlooked point is the relationship between risk and reward. The basic tenet of risk management is as fundamental as the laws of gravity: the rate of return should parallel the level of risk. In other words, the higher the risk, the higher should be the expected return.

This risk-return relationship is most evident in the bond market where, if a debt rating agency reduces the credit rating of an issuer, the yields on the bonds of that issuer rise in response to the heightened perception of risk. And here's the rub: the perception is often almost as significant as the actual risk itself.

In the summer of 2002, unexpectedly poor results by telecom leader Telus Corporation led to its debt securities being downgraded by Moody's to non-investment grade. Telus' bond prices plunged as investors shunned its now "junk-rated securities." The equity research analysts covering Telus were sufficiently unnerved to also drop their ratings, as a result of which Telus' shares also fell sharply. In the wake of this disappointment, the company was able to buy back its bonds at a significant discount. This debt reduction was financed by issuing new shares as investors warmly greeted the company's prudent balance sheet strengthening. The prices of Telus bonds and stocks recovered fully, its shares soaring by some 800% over the next three years.

An earlier example with less happy results would be of investors who bought technology stocks early in 2000 in the hope that the new era of technology would lift their fortunes, instead encountering a substantial decline in response to a heightened perception of risk that became substantial and lasting. Risk, whether perceived or real, is inescapable.

AN ALLY AND AN ADVERSARY

At worst, risk can dramatically, negatively and sometimes even permanently alter one's standard of living. This is why investors of all types need to spend time equating the accompanying risks with the associated opportunities. This is not to say you should run to the bedroom and stuff your life savings under the mattress, but to encourage you to recognize that, managed in a prudent manner, risk can be an ally, and that it can be offset by the potential rewards.

Think for a moment of the investors who snapped up shares of insolvent steelmaker Stelco in 2004. This was the year Stelco sought and was granted creditor protection. At the time, its shares were trading at the $1 level. By the spring of 2005, when the board announced it was spurning offers from would-be suitors, Stelco shares had soared to more than $4 per share, an impressive fourfold increase; a pretty neat trick for a company that was technically insolvent!

Don't Try This at Home

Don't take this as a recommendation to purchase shares of bankrupt businesses in the hope of a stellar turnaround. Turnarounds do happen, but the disappointments generally far outnumber the victories. It should be noted that the Stelco shares, which had climbed to as high as $4.48 in March of 2005, were back below the $1 level by mid-summer 2005. Take a moment to revisit the section in Chapter 2 entitled Falling Knives for more detail on why we generally tend to discourage this kind of bottom-feeding for perceived bargains.

THE MANY FACES OF RISK

Risk comes in many forms. Some are fairly benign, while others stand as a potentially deadly threat to your financial well-being. Nevertheless, it is possible to utilize investment strategies to safeguard against some of the more devastating types of risk. Our purpose with this chapter is to offer you some usable first aid rather than a medical degree on the vast topic of managing investment risk. You should emerge with a heightened level of awareness of the various forms of risk that can affect your portfolio, and with some time-tested strategies for managing risk in its various forms. If we impart just one message to you in this chapter it is that risk is an unavoidable yet manageable aspect of investing.

Here are some of the more common forms of risk that you are likely to encounter.

Market Risk

The type of risk that immediately springs to mind with most individual investors is that of the loss of capital, generally referred to as market risk. We've mentioned before how famous comedian Will Rogers used to worry not so much about the return *on* his investment, but the return *of* his investment. Many of the finer points on equity selection, where the market risk is generally thought to be greatest, have been covered in Chapter 8, so we won't repeat them here except to stress that it is possible to mitigate the degree of risk of capital loss by utilizing careful security-selection techniques.

One method of mitigating risk is to hold investments where there is a genuine concern over capital loss in a regular taxable investment account rather than in a registered non-taxable account such as an RRSP or a RRIF. Many investors make the mistake of holding their growth investments in their RRSPs in the belief that because equities should generally be assumed to be long-term investments, these investments should be made with long-term retirement savings. The flaw in this logic is that while capital gains realized inside a registered account are not subject to immediate taxation, there is no ability to utilize capital losses. In a non-registered account, capital losses can be carried back three years and carried forward indefinitely for the purpose of offsetting taxable capital gains.

Interest Rate Risk

Ever wonder why every word spoken by Alan Greenspan is so carefully scrutinized by professional investors, market watchers and the media? As chairman of the U.S. Federal Reserve Board, "the Fed," he has tremendous influence over the level of U.S. interest rates and, thanks to the widespread influence of the American economy, interest rate policies in much of the industrialized world.

You'd better believe that interest rates do really matter. Capital-intensive businesses that must raise large sums of capital on debt markets can have their fortunes significantly altered by increases and decreases in borrowing rates. Furthermore, the shares of companies such as financials and utilities that are considered to be interest-rate sensitive can face greater-than-normal share price volatility depending on the direction and speed of interest rate changes.

Though bonds are often mistakenly considered to offer risk-free returns, their value will fluctuate continually depending on the levels of interest rates prevailing over their lifespans. For investors who tend to hold their bonds all the way to maturity, these price fluctuations in value may not be of much concern. However, for those who need to liquidate bond holdings prior to maturity, price fluctuations can come as a rude awakening. As previously mentioned, bond prices have what is known as an inverse relationship to interest rate movements. When interest rates are on the decline, bond prices customarily tend to rise; when interest rates are on the rise, bond prices more often than not tend to fall.

Default Risk

Another risk to be found within the seemingly risk-free world of bonds is that of interest and/or principal default. When a bond is issued, the borrower pledges to make periodic payments of interest to the lender, the bond holder. This gives the bond holder a claim on the assets that comes before the stockholder in the event of bankruptcy. In many cases this claim is insufficient to safeguard a bond holder's principal, and in situations where the borrower is highly indebted a bond holder may be able to recoup only part of his or her original investment. Default risk, or credit risk, can mean less-than-expected bond returns, the shortfall ranging from an interruption of interest payments while a financially troubled borrower like Stelco reorganizes its financial commitments, to an outright loss of capital because of an insolvent borrower having substantially more liabilities than assets.

Bond rating agencies act much like credit agencies offering consumer credit ratings when someone applies for a loan. They compile volumes of statistics and work their way through a wide assortment of formulae to establish credit ratings on the debts of bond issuers. These ratings provide a signal of the degree of risk investors can expect from borrowers; the lower the debt rating, the higher the risk. This means, in turn, that riskier fixed-income investments should carry higher-than-average yields to compensate investors for taking on incrementally higher additional risk.

There are two major bond rating agencies in Canada: the Dominion Bond Rating Service (DBRS) and the Canadian Bond Rating Service (CBRS). The U.S. has three major agencies: Moody's, Fitch Ratings and Standard & Poor's. Below is a table that illustrates the classifications used by the two major Canadian bond rating services.

Credit Ratings and What They Mean

	DBRS	CBRS
Highest Quality	AAA	A++
Superior Quality	AA	A+
Good Quality	A	A
Medium Grade	BBB	B++
Lower Medium Grade	BB	B+
Moderately Speculative	B	B
Highly Speculative	CCC	C
In Default	CC	D
In Default/Low Liquidation Value	C	–

Source: Canadian Bond Rating Service, Dominion Bond Rating Service

Understanding a bond issuer's debt rating is of great importance in managing the degree of risk in what is ordinarily and mistakenly assumed to be the risk-free portion of portfolios. In fact, institutional investors such as pension plans usually set out in advance the minimum quality of debt instruments acceptable to their managers. In Chapter 13, we'll touch on the need for agreed-upon Investment Policy Statements, an important component of which is direction on the minimum acceptable quality as measured by debt ratings. Generally speaking, except for very short-term maturities, we prefer A-rated bonds or better in our clients' portfolios.

Opportunity Cost or Lost-Opportunity Risk

This form of risk deals not with what has happened, but with what has failed to happen. Lost-opportunity risk is perhaps best described as one of those "I could have kicked myself" moments when investors realize (always with the benefit of hindsight) that they sold a security too soon.

So what if Bernard Baruch, who gained notoriety for selling stocks well before they reached their peak, used to boast that he got rich by selling too soon. Who cares if profits from that recently sold investment continue to flow as freely as the beer at a stag party, but only for those who did not sell. Looking back with regret is costly and dangerous.

Of all the various forms of risk an investor can face, lost-opportunity risk is by far the most benign. This is particularly so as the lost ground can be made up by successfully reinvesting the proceeds of a premature sale in a new, bargain-priced investment, hopefully setting the stage for the next generation of profits.

Purchasing Power Risk—The Silent Killer

This form of risk is often the net result of not taking on enough risk in your investing habits, and is a particularly acute problem for investors accumulating assets to support themselves in their retirement years. Specifically, we're referring to the risk that someone who is blessed with tremendous longevity can see that blessing turn to a curse if their money is insufficient to support them in their later years. Over time, inflation will rob your money of some degree of its purchasing power. Stop to think, for example, of what it cost to mail a letter 10 or 20 years ago compared with today.

No doubt, rumours of the death of inflation have been greatly exaggerated. Mercifully, however, inflation in North America is not currently running at the breakneck pace of the 1970s and early 1980s; yet it remains with us still. It is precisely because of today's relatively tame rates of inflation that persistently rising prices are overlooked by investors planning their retirement. Low, single-digit inflation may not be particularly noticeable in a given year, yet the cumulative effect over what are an increasing number of retirement years for North American workers acts like a pounding surf continuously eating away at a coastline.

RISK MANAGEMENT

Every investor must be prepared to assume some modicum of risk in return for the kind of growth necessary to protect the long-term purchasing power of their invested dollars. Study after study has found that of all asset classes, equities offer the best inflation-protection qualities. Commensurate with equities' potentially greater reward is a proportionately greater degree of risk than is ordinarily found with other asset classes. Risk management is the art and science of striking the delicate balance between risk and reward—in equities perhaps most of all.

The following are some ways to manage risk in the equity portion of your portfolio.

STOP-LOSS ORDERS

A stop-loss order is an open order left with your broker to sell a particular stock should it fall to a specified price. It is placed below the prevailing market price, and its purpose is to set a floor price at which a falling security is to be sold. Just where that floor price should be is between you and your advisor. We recommend setting a stop-loss order at least 10% below the current market price for most blue chip securities. That way, ordinary daily fluctuations will be unlikely to trigger the stop-loss order, but a downward trend or a catastrophic event will. Stop-loss orders can be very useful in situations where there is the perceived risk of a sudden and dramatic fall in the value of a security. Having a stop-loss order in place will also help to remove some of the emotion surrounding a selling decision, because the decision to sell is, theoretically at least, made well in advance.

OPTIONS

An option is a financial instrument giving the holder the right to buy or sell an asset at a particular price for a specified period of time. Though they could be used for everything from real estate transactions to the drilling rights for an oil-rich property, we'll confine our comments on options to their use within a portfolio of common stocks.

There are two types of options: calls and puts. A call option entitles the holder to purchase shares at a fixed price for a fixed period of time; a put option entitles the holder to sell shares of a specific stock at a fixed price over a similarly fixed period of time. They are used by investors to hedge against making an inaccurate prediction on the direction of a stock's price.

Options can also be purchased for stock market indexes, meaning the same rationale could apply to investor expectations for the direction of an entire index or the market as a whole.

Calls

A call option can be used when an investor expects that a stock or an index is about to undergo a significant increase in value. For just a fraction of the value of the underlying investment, the right to purchase can be locked in for what it is hoped will be a substantial discount to the prevailing price at the time of the option's expiry. However, if the underlying stock or index drops in value, the investor would allow the option contract to expire because it would be "out of the money." The investor's loss would then be limited to the price paid for the option contract. It's for this reason that investors who use options consider them to be risk management tools.

Can You Take a Call?

Let's assume it's April and International Pumpernickel Inc. is trading at $5.75. An investor buys a call option, expiring in October, to purchase its shares for $6. The call costs 60 cents per option contract. If International Pumpernickel manages to climb to $9 before the option expires, the investor will have made a profit of $2.40. Here's how it would work:

The price of International Pumpernickel at the time of the option exercise	$9.00
minus	
The purchase price guaranteed by the option contracts	$6.00
equals	
The gain	$3.00
minus	
The purchase price of the option	$0.60
equals	
The net, pre-tax profit made by the investor	$2.40

An investor may choose to use a call option not only because of the mitigation of risk, but because of the aspect of leverage and its ability to magnify gains. Remember, in our example, the investor made $2.40 on a 60-cent investment. If the shares of International Pumpernickel had gone the other way, let's say dropping to $3 instead of rising to $9, the loss would have been limited to the 60 cents spent to purchase the call option, which would simply have been allowed to expire worthless.

Short Selling, Call Options and the Great Marble Rye Crisis

Short sellers will frequently use call options to protect themselves against a rapid appreciation in the value of a stock they are hoping will decline in value. You'll remember that short selling involves selling shares you don't own. Let's take another look at International Pumpernickel to illustrate the point.

Use Calls to Cover Your Assets

You've sold International Pumpernickel at $6 per share. If the stock drops to $3 you will have made a $3 per share profit! Now let's assume for a moment that you've shorted IP at $6. Thereafter, events turn terribly ugly. There's a marble rye crisis in Flyspeckia! Fearful of not being able to have a decent sandwich, residents begin hoarding loaves of International Pumpernickel's world-famous pumpernickel bread. Loaves are flying off store shelves faster than pre-election patronage appointments. Shares of International Pumpernickel soar, hitting a 52-week high of $9. Ordinarily, this would spell disaster for a short seller, but let's say you were also savvy enough to purchase IP call options for 60 cents apiece. You exercise your options, covering the short at the prescribed $6 called for in the option contract. Your loss has now shrunk from $3 per share to just 60 cents per share.

Covered Calls

Perhaps you already hold shares of IP, in which case you may opt to write a call on the stock in what is known as a covered call. Covered call writing is done to protect the shareholder against a decline in the underlying price of a given stock and to increase the yield on a portfolio. There are plenty of instances when an option contract will expire worthless for the purchaser.

To the seller, the premium received by writing the covered call contract is an attractive additional form of profit. Of course, it too is far from risk-free. If circumstances are such that the purchaser is "in the money," meaning that it is worth their while to exercise their call option, your shares of International Pumpernickel will be called away; that is, sold at the price predetermined in the call option contract. This really stings when the stock in question is experiencing strong share price growth. Theoretically, the loss from writing a covered call is unlimited. As such, treat this strategy as a risky endeavour usually best left to professionals who specialize in this area of investing.

Puts

A put option is a contract that gives the holder the right, but not the obligation, to sell a given stock at a particular price for a specified period of time. An investor would want to purchase a put option when expecting the price of a particular stock to fall. Let's use another imaginary titan of industry to illustrate the point.

Putting Your Foot Down

Shares of Catdiaper Industries are trading at $17.75. You, being the prescient investor that you are, have determined that its shares have an above-average probability of a serious drop in value. Hence, you purchase a put for $2.50 that entitles you to sell the stock for $14. If the stock drops as anticipated, you will be able to sell your put contract at a profit. However, if the shares of Catdiaper rise instead of fall, you, the holder of the put contract, will have to allow it to expire worthless and will lose the investment in the put. (All puts and calls have expiration dates.)

Buyer Beware

Puts and calls are useful risk-management tools widely used by investment professionals in their day-to-day activities. Be warned, however, that they are much more complex than they appear at first glance. Financial advisors who use options strategies require a special licence. Because of their costs, risks and complexity, in Canada, options strategies are offered by a relatively small number of advisors—and in our view it should stay this way.

HEDGE FUNDS

On the surface, it would seem that any discussion on hedge funds should be in the previous chapter, which was on equities. Our take on hedge funds is that if you wish to add them to your portfolio, it is best that they be treated as risk management tools above all else.

Hedge funds, also known as alternative investment funds, have been in existence for decades as investment vehicles that use a variety of strategies to achieve absolute returns for investors; that is, to realize positive rates of return during both rising and falling market conditions.

Due to the high minimum investment required by many hedge fund managers, this asset class remained something of an enigma to the majority of individual investors until very recently.

Originally, as their name suggests, hedge funds were meant to safeguard portfolios by building a hedge of financial protection around them. However, the 2000–2002 bear market saw them beginning to attract significant attention when most major market averages dropped in value, but a number of these funds managed to not only beat the market averages but also deliver real growth on their invested dollars. The painful lessons of Long-Term Capital Management's spectacular collapse of only a few years previously were rapidly being forgotten. Disillusioned with more traditional investment vehicles during what was a very tough period, investors once again began clamouring to get on the hedge fund bandwagon—a trend that has continued ever since.

Are alternative investment strategies appropriate for you? In a limited sense, they likely are. However, due to their very unusual DNA compared with more traditional investment vehicles such as mutual funds, great care must be taken to ensure you know what you are getting into. Hedge funds are a very wide-ranging field in which it is easy to get led astray. Hence, as they relate to you, they should be a means of safeguarding your portfolio's value by helping to manage risk.

A Vehicle—Not an Asset Class

Hedge funds are not an asset class in and of themselves. Instead, in much the same manner as mutual funds, they are a conduit through which an investor can access a wide assortment of investment styles and types of securities. And, as with mutual funds, hedge funds are not inherently speculative or conservative, excepting that they need to be narrowly defined for specific investment purposes.

Fish Gotta Swim, Birds Gotta Fly, I've Gotta Stick With This Mandate Until I Die

There is one specific and dramatic point of differentiation between traditional asset managers and the arguably less traditional practitioners of alternative asset management. One of the gravest sins a traditional asset manager can commit is that of style drift, an example of which would be when a value manager begins to hold stocks that would ordinarily be considered growth stocks. Another example would be when a large-cap equity manager winds up with a handful of small-cap stocks in the portfolio under his or her care.

Over the last 25 years, traditional asset management has experienced significant growth. As asset management, as a segment of the financial services industry, has grown and matured, there have been greater and greater degrees of specialization, some would say in direct response to both advancing technology and a marketplace demanding more precision as it becomes increasingly sophisticated. The more cynical view is that managers began to specialize in a bid to maintain a critical point of differentiation as the market for traditional asset management became increasingly crowded. Critics have contended that this increased specialization is nothing more than the kind of line extension one might see in the toothpaste aisle in their grocery store. We're not here to take sides. Nevertheless, we must admit that, while rigidly sticking to one's style mandate has its advantages with regard to the "know what you own" edict, a firm style mandate can also act as something resembling a straitjacket for an asset manager.

Recognizing this conundrum, investors are left with a choice: become more engaged in managing the managers to emphasize or de-emphasize certain styles according to shifting market conditions, or employ non-traditional asset managers to work alongside their more traditional compatriots. The net effect should be to reduce overall portfolio volatility (risk). This is the cornerstone of alternative investing.

The spectacular implosion of Long-Term Capital Management in 1998, together with the equally stunning collapse of Portus Alternative Asset Management in early-2005, serve as potent reminders that even securities that are designed to be used as risk management tools require proper care and due diligence in their selection. These two high-profile disasters should not drive you away from hedge funds as an investment vehicle. Instead, think back to some of the principles discussed in the last chapter. Know what you own. Monitor the investment's progress continually. Spread your risk among several securities. Give conscious thought to your own comfort level for risk. All of these homilies that are ordinarily reserved for stocks and mutual funds can and should apply with equal force to hedge fund investments.

The Past Is Not Always Prescient

As we outlined in the opening chapter, the 18-year bull market that began in 1982 and concluded in 2000 was unprecedented in its duration and magnitude. Though agreement is far from universal, there is a growing chorus who believe the next decade will be far less rewarding than the two that have gone before. For investors holding this belief, alternative investments carry much appeal.

In his March 16, 2005, *Wall Street Journal* column "Getting Going," Jonathan Clements gave a guarded endorsement for putting 10% of individual investor portfolios in alternative investment mutual funds (mutual funds that invest their assets in hedge funds).

Clements pointed to the distinct possibility that investors may face low market returns over the next 10 years or more. As such, he believes that a portfolio's performance should not be correlated with the broad U.S. stock market. (While the column was intended for a primarily American audience, we believe the same applies to Canadians.) Thus, any dramatic setback in the markets or their key indexes could be at least partially offset by alternative investments, in this way offering more consistency to the year-over-year performance of a portfolio employing these strategies.

Alternative investment mutual funds are, in Jonathan Clements's opinion, the preferred method for individual investors to gain access to some of the world's best hedge fund managers. He cites the higher degree of liquidity afforded by the mutual fund structure, which makes it easier for an individual investor of modest financial resources to get their money out of their portfolio. Hedge funds on their own typically have very limited liquidity provisions. The liquidity offered by alternative investment mutual funds gives investors an opportunity to rebalance their portfolios, something not available to large institutions and high-net-worth investors who can usually liquidate shares of their hedge funds only once per quarter and are sometimes required to give 30 days' or more notice of their intention to sell.

Clements had some very valid concerns about alternative investment mutual funds: the first, that there is not presently a very wide assortment of mutual funds utilizing alternative investment strategies as their primary mandate; the second, that the few that do troll the hedge fund waters tend to be quite expensive. The moral of the story as always: shop carefully.

Investors who purchase alternative investment funds place a tremendous amount of faith on the skills of the fund manager(s). A June 2004 study conducted by Merrill Lynch's Global Asset Allocation strategist Cesar Molinas found that most of the funds that his group studied failed to show significant performance gains relative to major market averages in both bull and bear markets. Molinas did concede that there was more evidence of excess returns in bear markets, precisely what the marketing literature of most hedge fund of funds claims they strive for. Molinas speculates in his report that the double layer of fees (management fee plus performance bonus) is one of the prime reasons for the lack of significant outperformance.

The whole point of hedge fund investing is to strip away the influence of the market and level the investor with the manager(s) skill. Without a doubt, the greatest risk in hedge fund investing is that the investor is saddled with an asset manager or managers whose skills are found to be wanting.

AS INEVITABLE AS DEATH AND TAXES

We've said it before in these pages but it bears repeating. We believe the handling of risk to be a rudimentary skill every serious investor must strive to master. Be forewarned, however, that achieving mastery over risk is as elusive as the famed Loch Ness Monster. Nevertheless, attempting to shun risk altogether is not an answer either. For the majority of the investors with whom we have had the pleasure of working, some degree of asset growth is a vital requirement to ensure long-term financial prosperity.

We are most likely going to live longer, more active lives than the generations that preceded us. The need to maintain purchasing power from your nest egg decades after you've collected your gold watch means assuming some degree of risk in order to achieve a necessary degree of growth. Taking steps to mitigate that risk is the answer. Seeking absolute safety of principal is understandable, but is not in itself a risk management strategy. In fact, a no-risk strategy could turn out to be exposing you to one of the greatest risks of all; the risk that you will outlast your money.

PART THREE

STAYING HEALTHY

CHAPTER 10

The Unfair Advantage

Using Reliable Research to Make Better Decisions

One of Bryan's passions is auto racing. His favourite race-car driver of all time, Mark Donohue, was remarkable for his ability to win races in all manner of cars. Donohue credited much of his success to an "unfair advantage" through a highly focused strategy and detailed preparation of the car in advance of a given race.

In a similar vein, Frank Clair won more Grey Cups than any other coach in Canadian football history. He was renowned for the hours he spent studying game films, as well as for putting his players through countless drills until they got the play being practised exactly right.

Michael is similarly reminded of a British officer whose meticulous preparation resulted in his commando group accomplishing their D-Day mission with scarcely a loss.

The moral of stories like these is simple: Don't leave any stone unturned. Prepare thoroughly, and your goal will become that much more attainable. Virtually all of the most successful and best-known investors from Warren Buffett to Benjamin Graham and Sir John Templeton to Kirk Kerkorian are noted for their aversion to unmanageable risk. None of these investment legends wants to be sidetracked by an unexpected turn of events, and all take great care to have as many facts available to them as possible before committing to an investment.

NO DARTBOARDS ALLOWED

While he certainly does not stand as a paragon of virtue, Gordon Gekko, the character played by Michael Douglas in the Oliver Stone film *Wall Street*, accurately summed up the attitude of true investors when he said, "I don't throw darts at a board. I bet on sure things."

The great Benjamin Graham sought his unfair advantage in correct *facts* and reasoning. His belief: get your facts right and you will be building your long-term strategy on a sound foundation. Our portfolios should likewise demand no less. Like Mark Donohue, Frank Clair and that D-Day commander, we should give ourselves an unfair investment advantage through meticulous preparatory research.

Michael counts himself privileged to have been in on the pioneering of investment research in Canada. However, his nostalgia about the ground-breaking 1960s quickly gives way to awe at the research tools today's investors have available to them compared with then.

Today, there is fingertip access to reliable, trustworthy information from every side, at every turn, at every level. On the corporate side, there are now separate investor relations executives and departments. Meetings and conferences are arranged to review latest results with covering analysts and interested professionals. "Guidance" is provided as to where future results are expected to fall. On the research coverage side, there is now a global army of investment professionals with the prestigious Certified Financial Analyst (CFA) designation. In addition, the media feature expert assessment and comment of every type, and the Internet has opened up a veritable Pandora's box of accessible investment-related information. Not only was there nothing like this before, but the whole research and related information process keeps getting better and better.

If there is a weakness, it is that the information available to today's investor can be almost overwhelming. Sadly, in rare occasions, it can also be calculatingly false and misleading, as witnessed by the sorry litany of fraud and deception that followed the bursting of the high-tech bubble. Miscreant corporations window-dressing ("faking" might be the better word) their earnings to meet publicized targets and to support their stock prices have become a highly undesirable part of the information and research process—taking unfair advantage in the worst sense.

Nevertheless, travesties like Enron and WorldCom only enhance what good research should be all about and is increasingly capable of providing. They have also taught us that interpretation, valuation and portfolio application are bridges all the more correctly crossed given the relevant facts. In due course, a great company will always ensure its own success. Unearth such a company early through accurate, fact-based research and the rest will take care of itself. Miss out on the basic facts and the risks of a poor investment will skyrocket. Protect yourself by digging a little, or have someone do the digging for you. The net result of your mining expedition could be a diamond in the rough.

This doesn't mean individual investors need to have the knowledge or tools of full-time investment research professionals. It does mean they shouldn't be deterred from acquiring at least some basic investment knowledge in their own interests. This way, they will be better equipped to ask their investment advisors pertinent questions and to follow what is being done on their behalf. The key is to have at least some knowledge of the very real advantages that reliable research can bring.

EMPIRICAL YOU

The older and more experienced Michael becomes, the more he believes in empirical observation to help arrive at one's own investment conclusions. Just as the distinguished Professor Frank Paish, under whom he gained his Ph.D., believed "housewives" are the best day-to-day economists, we can become our own best investors—not necessarily with expertise and the specialist knowledge we pay others to provide, but by keeping our eyes open, looking around us and asking logical questions from which helpful investment ideas might meaningfully flow.

ASKING WHY

Why is the economy supposed to be slowing down when shopping malls, flights, restaurants, and entertainment and sporting events are full? How can that housing bubble burst when construction continues unabated and carpenters, plumbers and skilled workers can't be found for love nor money? Why are high oil prices supposedly hurting so badly when city traffic remains clogged and gas-guzzling SUVs ever-popular? Why are corporations going out on merger and acquisition spres when the stock markets are supposed to be too expensive? Why shouldn't I be investing in companies that are being positively impacted by such activities and developments?

Questions like these will often leave investment advisors thinking too, and both investor and advisor could be agreeably surprised where they lead. They are questions that should also be asked in the knowledge that even the great investment managers can get their leads similarly.

Peter Lynch, the legendary retired manager of Fidelity's flagship Magellan Fund, always preferred kicking tires, knocking on doors and observing what went into shopping baskets to what economists or strategists could tell him. One of his memorable put-downs was that spending five minutes listening to an economist was to waste three. Mr. Lynch even liked linking potential investments to what children could draw with a crayon. Talk about a grassroots approach that worked—spectacularly!

Michael (with his training in economics) respectfully begs to differ with Mr. Lynch, and has always preferred to go about his research preparation and security selection in top-down fashion. By beginning with the global and Canadian economies, he feels he can better gauge whether the investment tides are flowing in and lifting all boats, flowing out and taking stock markets and supporting investment values down with them, or are at a choppy in-between stage which can spell added investment opportunity.

Opportunities abound, if you go about your research properly. This book began with a discussion on the massive bull market that was building in the white-knuckle summer of 1982. Twenty years later another recovery from an unexpectedly severe recession and bear market was also in the making. Today, standing out for the exceptional investment opportunities they provide are China's bursting on the world economic and investment stage, and the impressive turnaround in a debt- and deficit-ridden Canada that was next on the World Bank's stewardship list in the mid-1990s.

Another current example of empirical research is the watershed transition that is playing out in the all-important U.S. economy and investment marketplace, along with an accompanying adjustment in the U.S. dollar, still the world's premier reserve currency.

These are but some of the examples of prizes that are there for the taking by investors prescient enough to pick up on them ahead of the crowd. The resultant investment leg-up stands to be all the greater, and there will also be the escalating advantage from one of investment's oldest adages: "The trend is your friend."

You may not have the research and valuation capabilities of today's economists and investment experts, nor do you need to. However, what you can do to compensate for lacking the sophisticated tools of the professional investor is to ask the "right" questions through your own powers of observation; that is, do your own macro research. Here, too, you'd quickly find yourself in distinguished company; for example, Warren Buffett, whose legendary success is predicated on a simpler-the-better approach that everyone can understand.

KNOW WHAT YOU OWN

We commented previously on Buffett's refusal to invest in high-tech because he and his partner Charlie Munger couldn't understand it. However, they have never had any problem with basic activities such as chocolates, paint, bricks, underwear, jewelry, furniture, newspapers and mobile homes, with which the Berkshire Hathaway group is liberally stocked. Their overriding requirement is to be sure of what they are investing in. It's a need that is also reflected in their inclination to pass up an investment opportunity when there is something in an annual report or corporate communiqué they cannot understand. This doesn't preclude them from having views on investment-sensitive topics like the U.S. economy, the U.S. dollar, interest rates, energy developments, or gold and precious metals, to mention some of their recent hobby horses—views that become reflected in their selections and the prices they are prepared to pay for what they know they are investing in.

We have every right to ask questions like these of our investment advisors. The resultant top-down, macro-to-micro impact on our portfolios can only be all the more beneficial as a result.

IT'S THE SELECTIONS THAT COUNT

Regardless of the approach, investment ultimately boils down to choosing individual stocks and equity products with which to build required longer-term wealth in superior fashion; in other words, to a bottom-up or micro selection of securities. Thorough research is all-important at this point-of-entry stage, whether by dint of our own efforts—direct or indirect, rudimentary or sophisticated—or with the help of others. Or, perhaps better still, through a combination of outside expertise and our own individual ideas.

NOTHING BEATS CORRECTLY ASSESSING THE FUNDAMENTALS

The table that follows illustrates the basic research approach Michael has always favoured. Filling in a summary questionnaire like this is not difficult; you could do it too, and in the process equip yourself with revealing answers to many key investment considerations.

QUESTIONS AND ANSWERS

Below are some of the typical questions we like to get answers to before making a decision to invest in the shares of a company.

- How have sales or revenues grown?
- Has this growth accelerated or decelerated?
- Have bottom-line earnings grown faster or more slowly than revenues?
- What do profit margins reveal about management's effectiveness?
- How adequate are the cash flows through the company, and how have they grown?
- How strong is the balance sheet? To what extent is it leveraged by debt?
- What have the returns been on the common shareholders' equity, and how do they compare with others in the same field?
- How have the stock markets rated results?

It's all the better when data like this can be measured over a period as long as 10 years, during which there will likely have been both up and down cycles, not to mention other assorted challenges for management. Thus, a rising trend over the period being analyzed should be construed favourably; even better, if the annual growth rates and profit ratios are higher over the second half than the entire period; and best of all if they are highest in the very latest year. If the statistics don't measure up this way, start asking why. You'll simply need to dig more deeply before making any final decision. Successful investing is no mistake, and it has little or nothing to do with luck.

Given today's plethora of freely available information, it shouldn't be difficult to obtain basic information for the required rudimentary analysis. A latest annual report is invariably the best source. Warren Buffett devours annual reports from all over, and tells how he gets great ideas for investment from them. At the very

RESEARCH SUMMARY QUESTIONNAIRE
(absolute numbers in millions)

Consolidated Income Statement	Latest Year	Previous Year	5 Yrs Ago	10 Yrs Ago	Annual Growth (or changes)		
					Latest	5 yrs	10 yrs
Revenue							
Operating Income/Profit							
Net Income/Earnings							
Dividends							
Cash Flow							

Consolidated Balance Sheet

Total Assets

Working Capital
(Current Assets–Current
  Liabilities)

Long-Term Debt

Shareholders Equity

Total Capital
Debt: Total Capital (ratio)

Share Data

Earnings Per Share
- Basic
- Diluted (if applicable)

Cash Flow Per Share

Dividends Per Share
Payout %

Equity (Book Value) Per Share
Return on Equity (ROE)

General

Share Price (year-end)
Shares Outstanding
Market Capitalization
  (price × shares)
Price-Earnings Ratio
  (annual average)

least, the annual report, particularly the pages containing management's own discussion and analysis, will be worth a cursory leaf-through. All annual reports include a summary of past results, usually for five years and sometimes, preferably, for 10. If the summary doesn't go this far back, ask the corporate secretary or investor relations department to provide you with the numbers you need.

In due course you might well become sufficiently expert to "eyeball" annual reports and summaries for the answers being sought. Or, to be that much more sure, you might find it easier to set up a basic spreadsheet on your home computer for regular updating.

You might also come to the stage where you want to compare and measure companies you are considering with others in the same industries. This would be highly commendable. After all, superior investing is a relative affair that we should all be obliged to measure up to. This way, you'll be able to establish where the best relative investment values lie.

No matter how rudimentary, there is no better discipline than fundamental analysis along basic lines like these. Ultimately, it will enable you to gauge how bottom-line earnings and returns on shareholders' equity are faring, and whether or not they are being adequately reflected in the share price. EBITDA (earnings before interest, taxes, depreciation and amortization), alpha-beta analysis and other refinements can come later. Our experience teaches us that it is most often best to keep it simple.

As his measure, Warren Buffett compares the annual gain in the Berkshire Hathaway per-share book value with the corresponding total return on the benchmark S&P 500 Index. When the Berkshire gain is higher, he feels he has done his job; when it is lower, he feels his efforts have been lacking.

Michael still prefers filling in rudimentary tables and going about his research the old-fashioned way for the essential "feel" this gives him. However, by all means develop *your* way to become *your* own best research analyst. Most likely you'll want some outside help in the process; so much the better if this adds to the awareness of what good research can ultimately bring.

FEELING THE PULSE

Discipline yourself to stick to it, and even the simplest research approach will soon lead to the ability to feel the pulse of companies you are considering or have invested in. You'll also come to identify when the pulse rate speeds up or slows down, and whether changes (good or bad) are being signalled.

In essence, this is what technical analysis (and research) is all about, whether charting the tempo in the markets as a whole, or in plotting relevant dots, lines and patterns in different sectors and stocks making up the markets. Connect the dots and/or draw the lines between different points on stock and market charts, and the resultant patterns can often be highly revealing.

Thus, respective lines drawn through annual peaks or annual lows can highlight important up or down trends. Similarly, lines connecting past annual lows can indicate support levels for future buying, while lines drawn through past peaks can highlight ceilings needing to be penetrated for any sustained upside breakout.

Moving-average lines based on closing prices over a succession of a set number of days are another widely watched—and used—technical indicator. When this average is calculated on periods as long as 150 or 200 days at a time, the moving-average price line can also be indicative of longer-based trends. It's always a comforting sign if prices remain above the moving-average line through periods of market turbulence; on the other hand, prices falling through their moving-average line can often signal further weakness to come.

Like its fundamentally-based counterpart, technical research can be as sophisticated or basic as you want. Whatever your approach, it's much better than reading tea leaves. Go about it in a consistent, disciplined fashion and, like technical analysts, you too will come to learn how to feel the pulse.

THE KITCHEN TABLE ANALYST AND OTHER APPROACHES

Michael will always remember the gentlemanly Bob Farrell of Merrill Lynch, one of the all-time great technical analysts, telling him of the handful of key charts he filled in by himself on the family kitchen table. There's a lesson for us all when Wall Street's top market technician, with his own budget and support staff, nonetheless liked keeping his finger on the pulse in this most homespun of ways.

In his days as a bank analyst, Michael used to routinely plot the prices of bank shares one against the other. An admittedly apples-to-oranges comparison helped alert him to which shares were more active and less active, which were growing the most and the least, and where the better relative values might lie. It wasn't mathematically pure, but it helped him keep his finger on the pulse of a key sector in the Canadian financial markets.

Tony Fuergeson, another Wall Street veteran Michael knows and respects, likes to note the percentage increase in the annual dividend, usually made at the same point each year along with one of the quarterly declarations. If the percentage increase is the same as the previous year, he takes it as a sign that all is continuing well; if higher than previously, that the company anticipates doing better; if lower, that there could be difficulties ahead.

Others believe the consolidated balance sheet is where the true heartbeat of a corporation is to be found. We commented earlier on how Warren Buffett measures Berkshire Hathaway's progress in terms of the annual increase in shareholders' equity. Benjamin Graham used to look for changes in working capital and that part of working capital held in cash or liquid form. Here, too, develop your own criteria, and follow them in disciplined fashion.

THE *ETHICAL* UNFAIR ADVANTAGE

At the everyday level, it's also worth carefully going through your monthly or quarterly statements, if only to develop a feel for the individual holdings in your portfolios and, from these, for how your portfolio is doing on the whole. Even a regular daily or weekly scan of the closing prices of the stocks and fund products making up your portfolio will help you develop an experienced eye to add to the unfair advantage and the better decision-making that reliable research always brings.

Regularly feeling the pulse can tell a revealing story. Doctors and nurses do it as a matter of good practice; we investors should do it too.

MAZE OR LABYRINTH?

Research can often end in what seems a blind alley or a cul-de-sac. This doesn't necessarily mean it has been wasted. Rather than being discouraged, you should then ask the key question of whether these efforts have led into a maze or a labyrinth—much better the latter than the former.

Mazes are defined as blind alleys and wrong turns set up to deceive and defeat. Labyrinths, by contrast, are likened to a single journey with lots of twists, turns and obstacles that sometimes seem to take one far off course but ultimately turn out to be trustworthy paths leading successfully to the desired destination.

Research by definition involves exploring the unknown, the risk versus reward aspect of investing. However, go about it thoroughly and the chances will be greatly increased of successfully travelling a road that could seem labyrinthian at certain points, but will nonetheless lead all the more surely to sought-for investment goals.

Many decades ago, Winston Churchill implored Franklin Delano Roosevelt to give his war-weakened nation the tools to finish the job of defeating the Nazis. We investors need tools too—research tools, which are available to us as never before, as basic or as sophisticated as we want.

In the summer of 1975, shortly before his death, Benjamin Graham concluded an article on "The Future of Common Stocks" with a slight twist on a quote that Virgil, his favourite poet, had directed to Roman farmers of his day, but that Graham suggested could apply equally to equity investors of his time: "O enviably fortunate investors, if only you realized your current advantages." One such advantage was the developing investment research of that period. Think of the scale and the sophistication with which it is available now.

Whether you are an everyday investor, a financial planner or an investment advisor, don't be afraid to demand the facts, to ask intelligent questions and to dig as simply or as deeply as you want or are able. In other words, it matters not whether you perform the number crunching yourself or if you rely upon an analyst to do it for you, so long as you have at your disposal an accurate set of facts that will enable you to make well-informed investment decisions. Don't be ashamed to follow the "kiss" (keep it simple, stupid) principle in laying that all-important research foundation. After getting started, you might well find yourself wanting to learn more than your beginner's research, in which case the Canadian Securities Institute has much to help you to the next stage. Who knows, you might even become sufficiently hooked to end up with the coveted Chartered Financial Analyst designation!

Whatever your choice, there *is* an unfair advantage to be gained by making better decisions with reliable research—to spot opportunities as they emerge and to identify trends that warn of gathering risk.

CHAPTER 11

Pay to Play

Fees and Commissions

THE GRAND ILLUSION

For more than two decades, many Canadian investors have been under a grand illusion that when it comes to the management of their portfolios, they could enjoy the financial equivalency of a free lunch. It's an illusion that first materialized in the late 1980s with the advent of the deferred sales charge on mutual fund purchases.

Up to that point, the overwhelming majority of mutual fund purchases had been paid for with upfront ("front-end") fees that were relatively high compared with today's standards. The deferred sales charge, or DSC ("back-end" fees), meant that the commission paid to purchase a mutual fund was buried among the fund's management fees and expenses. Investors would be liable for an exit fee were they to pull out their money within a specified period of time, after which the exit fees would disappear.

The illusion was that if you just stayed invested long enough, you had executed an investment free of commissions. The reality, of course, was and is that nothing is free and that managers instead charged fees and expenses directly through what has come to be known as the management expense ratio (MER).

SOMETHING FOR NOTHING

As the markets continued their upward spiral through the 1990s, discount brokerages waged intense price wars to attract the growing population of do-it-yourself investors. Some of the most creative minds in advertising launched elaborate campaigns designed to attract these investors into the do-it-yourself arena. More often than not, these campaigns addressed the issue of cost, yet the issue of value was obscured. Rapidly rising markets provided a veritable tailwind for investors, resulting in many abandoning long-established investment practices and counsel in favour of what they hoped would be quick and massive gains. The old investment industry adage "never confuse a bull market with brilliance" was dismissed as just another relic of a bygone era. The crushing blow of reality that was the 2000–2002 bear market reasserted the enduring wisdom of that maxim and shook some do-it-yourselfers back to financial advisors.

Today, specially structured investment products are the latest incarnation of the grand illusion. This is not meant to demean structured products, a term that covers a popular and fairly wide assortment ranging from hedge fund-of-fund vehicles to equity-linked notes to closed-end funds and more. The thread linking this divergent group is that most are offered as new issues, and when a new issue is purchased, the commission earned by the advisor is paid by the issuer, not the client—not directly at least. Once again, investors are left with the impression they are receiving something for nothing, furthering the grand illusion that they can have their money professionally managed, yet paid for by someone else.

As large numbers of investors become more experienced and develop more sophisticated investment needs, demand for greater value from the providers of financial products and services should, and does, follow. Intense competition for market share has led to yet another example of creative destruction, as new investment offerings aim to bring increased transparency and cost efficiency to the investment process for the individual investor.

There was a time, not all that many years ago, when stocks could be purchased only through a licensed stockbroker. Full retail commissions were applied to each and every trade regardless of whether or not advice was dispensed or needed. Today, the range of discount brokerage services is extensive, as many of the leading firms compete by offering value-added services rather than more traditional recommendations for their attractive prices.

A similar strategy is underway at full-service investment firms, with firms seeking to compete against each other on the basis of value-added services. Good trade execution, competent research and friendly staff have come to be regarded as a commodity. Now, firms and their advisors are adding to their already extensive array of products and services to differentiate themselves from what at times can be a fairly homogeneous and highly competitive field. Insurance products have been added to the menu of offerings at most full-service investment houses. Advisors are being taught to act as the financial equivalent of a family doctor, referring clients to specialists as required.

COST VS. VALUE

Oscar Wilde once famously wrote that a cynic is "a man who knows the price of everything and the value of nothing." Much of the criticism that has been levelled at the financial services industry has been centred (in many cases justifiably so) on the issue of cost. The matter of value is prone to more subjective measurement, and all too often very little attention is paid to it.

Throughout *Portfolio First Aid* we've asked you to undertake some serious soul-searching to understand what you want to achieve through investing. We've also asked you to give serious consideration to the amount of time you are realistically able to commit to your investments, and your level of expertise and real interest in acquiring more investment knowledge. Once you have reached a point where you are able to articulate what you want, you can progress to finding out who or what can help you achieve these goals. This is where the issue of value enters the picture.

A Little Self-Analysis Now Can Reduce the Risk of Disappointment Later

Here are five questions you need to ask yourself to help determine if you should or should not be a do-it-yourselfer:

- Do I want financial planning help?
- Where am I going to get my investment ideas from, and should I have someone making recommendations to me?
- Do I want to be involved with the day-to-day investment decision-making, or should I turn it all over to a portfolio manager?
- Who is going to monitor the portfolio and how often?
- How much time am I prepared to give the ongoing research necessary for the effective running of my portfolio?

How much you spend on the proper care and feeding of your portfolio is dependent in large part on the degree of professional help you want to have.

VALUE-ADDED SERVICES FROM THE DISCOUNTERS

For the do-it-yourself investor, the focus is usually primarily on the cost element, yet here too, value is an important consideration. While discount brokers do not offer advice, their ability to perform accurate and timely trade on execution is of great importance. During the tech stock rally of the late 1990s, one of Canada's most popular discount brokerages experienced tremendous difficulty in keeping up with the burgeoning demand for service from its clientele because it had not anticipated or prepared itself for such a surge in demand. The result was a rash of disgruntled customers, some of whom moved their business to smaller competitors who charged slightly higher trading commissions, yet were able to execute orders quickly.

The value proposition for a do-it-yourselfer should not be limited to trade capabilities. Many of Canada's leading discount brokerages are affiliated with major full-service brokerages and investment banks. Does your discount broker offer you access to its parent company's research library? What about financial planning tools? These are just two of the features of a full-service brokerage that will often also cross over to the discount channel as value-added services.

HOW "FULL" IS YOUR FULL-SERVICE BROKER?

The competition among full-service brokers for your business is extremely intense. Advisors at these firms work hard to differentiate themselves by taking on additional service staff (usually at their own expense) to offer financial planning assistance to clients and more of a personalized approach than their nearest competition.

At the head office level, full-service brokerages are constantly trying to differentiate themselves from their competitors through a variety of means, some of which include:

- publishing up-to-date research reports on a wide range of stocks, trusts, REITs, mutual funds, etc.
- employing market strategists to assist their advisors in positioning client portfolios
- offering exclusive access to third-party investment managers
- having estate planning professionals on staff to assist clients
- tying investment accounts to credit cards and lines of credit in a bid to capture both the assets and liabilities columns of a client's personal balance sheet

ASSET-BASED FEES

The latest incarnation of the cost/value continuum is asset-based pricing, which is a nice way of saying fees. A fee-based investment account is one where a client chooses to pay his or her advisor a flat fee for service rather than commissions every time a purchase or sale is transacted.

The most significant advantage to an investor of moving from paying commissions to an asset-based fee is the heightened transparency that the fee brings to the client-advisor relationship. Even though you may have been working with your advisor for many years and have built a relationship on a solid foundation of trust, it is not at all unusual, in fact it's likely human nature, to occasionally wonder if some trades are being recommended for the sake of the portfolio or for the pay packet of the advisor who may need to generate some commission revenue, particularly as month end approaches. If your advisor is being paid a flat fee, much of the natural suspicion of conflicted interests is eliminated.

Just as investors are freed from paying trading commissions when their portfolios are subject to a fee, this method of paying for financial services enables investors to purchase mutual funds that are not ordinarily no-load funds on a no-load basis. In addition, access is granted to "F" class mutual funds, which are identical to their front- and back-end load fund cousins with the exception that the management expense ratio is reduced, in many cases by as much as 50 basis points (0.50%). This is because the fund company has stripped out the ongoing compensation normally paid to advisors because "F" class funds are only available for purchase in fee-based accounts.

Fixed-income purchases within a fee-based account also receive preferential treatment. When an investor purchases a bond from his or her broker, the commission is not stated in the same manner as a stock purchase or the load on a mutual fund. The broker's commission is the spread between the wholesale price of the bond and the "net to client" or NTC price of the bond. In a fee-based account, bond purchases are made at the wholesale price, which can boost the bond's yield by usually anywhere from half to three-quarters of a percentage point.

Out of the Shadows

Depending on how you invest, there can be significant cost savings in pursuing a fee-based relationship with your advisor rather than the more traditional pay-as-you-go, commission-based method. Beyond the cost savings, there is something less tangible yet of equal or perhaps even greater value: the true cost of managing your portfolio emerges from the shadows, allowing you to make a more accurate evaluation of whether you are receiving value for the fees paid to manage your portfolio.

The Benefits Are Not Universal

Not everyone should be in a fee-based program. For some investors, a pay-as-you-go, commission-based structure will prove to be the better value. These are investors who would ordinarily have very few transactions occur in their portfolio. Thus, an investor with a portfolio largely made up of bonds, preferred shares and high-yielding, blue-chip common stocks that will be held for a long time would tend to fit the profile of someone whose needs are likely to be better served by having a commission-based portfolio.

Just the Facts, Ma'am

How should you make the determination whether a fee-based program is right for you? The best way we've found is to begin by taking a hard look at your past investment habits. We suggest that you needn't analyze any more than three years in the life of your portfolio. Add up what you have paid in commissions, mutual fund loads, RRSP or RRIF trustee fees, as well as any other fees that may have been tossed into the mix over that 36-month period. Don't forget to add in the MER on any mutual funds that you hold or held during the period under review. All of the information, with the exception of the mutual fund MERs, will be found on your monthly or quarterly investment statements. These latter costs are readily obtained by calling either your advisor or the fund companies themselves, or by looking up the fund through an online service such as Globefund (www.globefund.com).

Once you have the total of what you have paid, divide that number into the 36-month average value of the account(s) in question and multiply by 12 to arrive at an average annual cost. The net result will be a percentage that can then be compared against the annual fee an advisor will quote for managing your portfolio. The fee will be quoted in terms of an annual percentage of your assets under administration with your advisor. This will make for a relatively easy "apples to apples" comparison.

Asset Based Fee Pricing vs. Traditional Commission Model

Analysis for John Smith
Period of Aug. 30/01 to Aug. 30/04

Portfolio Value as of Aug. 30, 2004 $328,500

Current Costs	Percentage	Annually	Fee based	Percentage	Annually	Monthly
MER on Mutual Funds	2.54%	$3,755	Blended Fee	1.33%	$4,369	$364
Commissions	1.22%	$3,685				
Registered Acct Fee		$133	Less Tax Deduction	0.64%	$2,097	$174
Non-deductible		$0				
Net Fee	2.31%	$7,573.00	Net Fee	0.69%	$2,272	$190

Estimated Total Annual Savings After-Tax $5,301

Notes:

MER is the annual Management Expense Ratio charged on all Mutual Funds and is expressed as an average of your existing funds

Commissions are on equities only and are quoted as an average over the last 36 month period

Calculation of Tax Deduction assumes a marginal tax rate of 48%

The Net Fee is calculated as the total of all current fees expressed as a percentage of the current Portfolio Value

Virtually all the fee-based programs offered by Canadian firms today offer discounts on a sliding scale in a bid to encourage investors to consolidate all their investment holdings with the firm. It is for this reason that if you and your spouse have several investment accounts, you should conduct the 36-month review on all of the accounts and then ask for a fee quote based on the amassed total.

Another Pricing Option

Most of the major investment houses in Canada offer the choice of having a blended fee or a flat fee. A flat fee is, as the name implies, charged as a percentage of your total assets under administration. A blended fee, on the other hand, charges different fees for fixed-income and equity investments; the fee for fixed income will be smaller than the fee for equities. A more conservative investor would stand to benefit over a more aggressive growth style of investor as the conservative investor is likely to hold a greater percentage of fixed income investments in his or her portfolio than their growth-oriented counterpart.

If you are worried that to gain a higher fee the advisor may recommend a more aggressive, equity-driven strategy than you need, the blended fee is not right for you. It should be noted, though, that if you are entering into a relationship with an advisor and the core value of trust is not present, then maybe you need to rethink the decision to enter into that relationship in the first place.

Investment Counsellors

Virtually all investment counsellors charge fees as a percentage of assets. Their rates are usually less than half the expense ratios of mutual funds but, as you will recall from Chapter 4, are only more suitable for higher net-worth investors.

One additional benefit with investment counsellors are that their fees are tax deductible if they are charged for an account that is not registered; that is, a regular cash or margin account as opposed to a RRSP or RRIF. This is in marked contrast to brokers where fees are not tax-deductible.

KEEP ON SMILIN'

Suppose you've done your analysis and found you can save money by moving from pay-as-you-go commissions to a fee-based method of compensating your advisor. The markets are rising, and so is your portfolio. The schoolboy grin on your face is rivalled only by those on the apparently very happy men on television in the

Viagra ads. Will you keep on smiling, though, if the markets enter a protracted period of decline?

It's easy to spot the value when your portfolio is growing, but how wide will that smile be if you're paying to watch your portfolio decline in value? Remember, just as a rising market tide lifts all portfolios, a falling market will exert a reverse influence. This is the time when your advisor can really earn his or her fees by limiting the slide of your portfolio's value. This is the essence of relative versus absolute performance, a subject we will explore in the next chapter.

While it is reasonable to expect your advisor to work even harder on your behalf when markets are falling rather than rising, it is unreasonable for those in a fee-based model to abandon the model simply because they can no longer discern the advantage accruing to them. In many respects, your advisor is an employee and you are the employer. If you want to have advisors working as hard or harder for you than anyone else, don't make the mistake of radically changing the compensation model at the time when you need them the most. If your advisor is not doing the job you expect, don't take half measures. Replace an inadequate advisor with someone who is willing and able to do the job.

APPLES AND ORANGES

Much has been written over the last decade decrying the level of fees charged by mutual fund companies as reflected in their MERs. The comparison often made to index funds and/or exchange traded funds, however, this is a little like comparing apples and oranges. We're not here to apologize for the Canadian mutual fund industry or to castigate it. We are always prepared to pay for performance. If a particular mutual fund is delivering only market returns in good and bad markets then maybe the managers are not earning their keep. Before making that determination, though, we would want to be certain we were evaluating its performance in the proper context.

Index funds and exchange-traded funds are what are known as passively-managed investments. No daily buy or sell decisions are made by the fund manager. Instead, this type of investment mirrors the entire market index or, in the case of exchange-traded funds, a specific sub-index. Because there is no ongoing management, the cost structure of this type of investment is much lower than that found even with "F" class mutual funds. It is not unusual for the fee savings on an actively managed mutual fund to be 65% to 75% of the MER of an "F" class fund.

The quid pro quo is that active management decisions, such as how much exposure to have to a market sector, or for that matter to the equity markets altogether, are left to the investor. An actively managed mutual fund will take some, if not all, of the burden of that responsibility off of your shoulders but, as you might expect, will only do so at a cost. This brings us back to the issue of value. If a fund manager can make ongoing decisions better than you could on your own with an index fund, they will have added value and are, in our view, worth the price paid. If the performance is not there, assuming of course that the performance criteria are clearly understood, you've got some decisions to make.

FEE-ONLY PLANNERS

There is a small but hardy breed of advisors who do not invest any of their clients' money. In fact, they seldom, if ever, recommend specific securities. These are fee-only financial planners who more often than not are accountants and/or certified financial planners. As part of a suite of services for the clients they serve, these advisors will work to construct a detailed asset allocation strategy as part of a detailed Investment Policy Statement. Their appeal is that because they do not represent any one mutual fund company, or stand to benefit from the purchase of one type of asset versus another, their advice is deemed to be unbiased.

Fee-based planners will on occasion bill by the hour but, in our experience, most will quote a flat fee for their services. The fee-based advisor approach can work well when the client is on a flat fee with a full-service brokerage, using the plan drawn up by the fee-only advisor as a blueprint to guide the broker in security selection. However, the process can become quite costly if the client pays a fee to the fee-only advisor and then turns to a full-service advisor, paying commissions on transactions. Some do-it-yourself investors will utilize the services of a fee-only advisor to draw up the plan, and then use a discount broker to execute the strategy.

One major concern regarding fee-only advisors haunts us, and it is that because fee-only planners are not engaged in daily, hands-on dealing with securities, there is a tendency to take a rather academic approach to portfolio construction. Many investors who have used the services of a fee-only planner do not have an ongoing relationship with the planner. Remember that investing is a process, not an event. Markets are dynamic by nature, as are client needs and expectations. Even the best-laid plans, not just the securities in the portfolio that result from the plan, require regular review and updating. It is for this reason that investors should engage the services of a fee-only planner only if they are willing to enter into a long-term relationship.

NO FREE LUNCH

You probably learned long ago, and we've mentioned it numerous times, that there is no such thing as a free lunch. There are costs associated with the management of a portfolio regardless of whether you use the services of professional management or you are a hands-on, do-it-yourself type of investor. The quest to reduce the cost of investing is very necessary, because any resulting savings will flow straight to your bottom-line profit. Do not, however, lose sight of the essential element of value. Take the time to think about the level of support you want and need. That is always a good starting point.

CHAPTER 12

What's Your Number?

Benchmarking Performance

Setting benchmarks against which you can measure, over time, the progress of your portfolio is an area of investing that often sends investors down blind alleys, ultimately resulting in inaccurate or inappropriate investment decisions. In this chapter, we will examine the measurement of portfolio performance from two distinct vantage points. The first takes a financial planning approach. The investor (or their advisor) works from the future to the present, and following a series of detailed calculations arrives at an average compounded rate of return necessary to meet long-range objectives. In some sense, this approach is comparable to golfers focused on lowering their handicap, unconcerned with the scores of others in their foursome.

The second approach to benchmarking performance takes on, by comparison, more of an immediate tone. It is, to once more use the golfing analogy, somewhat like tournament play: keeping score in a game against one or more opponents. In some sense, your aims for your portfolio may be comparable to playing in a Pro-Am Tournament. You would love to be able to brag of beating the Pro, but the reality is that you are really striving to remain within striking distance of the Pro's score.

FAIL TO PLAN—PLAN TO FAIL

Inevitably, we all reach the stage in our life where we have to spend some serious time determining whether we are going to have enough to sustain ourselves in the manner we would like in what should be the sunset rather than the twilight of our ever-lengthening lives.

We may determine that there are many adjustments to be made to enjoy the sunset. We will be able to make some without too much fuss, like selling the family home for something smaller and cheaper once the children have moved out. (Some might suggest that this should be done immediately once the last child has left the nest to ensure there is no return trip!) Dropping a seldom-used club membership and getting by with only one family car are other tactics readily used by retirees to conserve capital. But what if we've cut back and downsized and still lack the capital for the Sunbelt time-share we were going to commit to? And what of those travel plans we had someday hoped to fulfill? For those who have had the misfortune to fall into poor health, rising health-related costs only add to the concerns. No one wants to depend on their children for financial support in their later years. What a scary thought that our main retirement problem could become living too darn long!

There is undoubtedly a lot to keep all of our minds concentrated on sobering thoughts like these. It's also far better that these thoughts happen sooner rather than later, leaving enough time to undertake an individualized savings and investment program aimed at ensuring that ultimate "margin of safety" the great Benjamin Graham regarded as imperative—or the moat that his disciple Warren Buffett repeatedly emphasizes as a measure of portfolio protection.

Let's face it, we shouldn't want to be beholden to government support programs in an era of rising longevity, taxes at very turn and soaring health costs. A recent study conducted for the American Association of Retired Persons (AARP) concluded that the U.S. social security system could run out of money in the early 2040s, a decade when it is estimated over 70 million people will be counting on it as their main source of retirement income. In Canada, the Canada Pension Plan mercifully appears to be in better shape. We also have our Old Age Security program. Nevertheless, their solvency will be increasingly tested as a rising proportion of the Canadian population enters retirement. The fact that the mighty General Motors and other major corporations are facing increasingly unmanageable commitments to their pensioners only adds to future retirement worries. Instead, let's concentrate on providing for our own *independent* retirement futures through timely, personalized, wealth-building investing.

WHAT'S THE SCORE?

You've likely heard of cooperative games where no one keeps score. Supposedly, they foster team spirit and protect fragile egos from soul-crushing defeat at executive retreats and in the kindergarten classroom. (Do you really need us to make the painfully obvious joke here?) These games are more than a little reminiscent of the *Seinfeld* episode where George and Jerry are at a woman's apartment for a party to celebrate the New York marathon and cheer on the runners. Just as George finishes proclaiming himself to be "king of the idiots," the party host leans from her window to greet the runners, screaming a full-throated "You're all winners." With exquisite timing, Jerry turns to George and says, "Suddenly, a contender for the throne emerges."

Call us a couple of knuckle-dragging, unenlightened, slack-jawed mouth-breathers, but we want to know the score. You need to know the score, particularly when it comes to your financial situation. Are you winning or losing? We don't like to lose, and will work twice as hard to avoid the sting of defeat as to savour a victory. We're pretty certain that when it comes to your portfolio you feel pretty much the same. How will you ever know if you are ahead or behind if no one is keeping score?

This, in fact, is what *Portfolio First Aid* is all about: diagnosing what is wrong, prescribing what to do toward an investment goal like secure retirement and staying financially healthy. An essential three-part process will become progressively easier with at least some basic investment knowledge, the provision of which is another purpose of this book. In addition, your personalized investing will need to be quantified and measured as you proceed down that retirement road aided and abetted by a portfolio of financial assets designed to last longer than you do.

RETIREMENT CALCULATIONS

Later in this chapter we will focus on benchmarking portfolio performance as part of the accompanying accountability that will also be essential. Clearly, the time available will be vital in determining how your retirement portfolio should be balanced between fixed income and equities, as well as the degree of risk that it can prudently be exposed to. The more time there is, the more compounding will be able to work its magic, and the lower will be the overall goal attainment risks. Conversely, the less time to work with, the greater the risks and the higher the likelihood of enforced retirement adjustments.

Considerations like these will help you draw your own personalized road map to retirement. They will also set the stage for the ultimate question every investor should be called upon to answer, ideally with the help of their financial advisor. In full, the question involves how much you need your portfolio to grow in order to retire in the style you would like, and what the necessary average rate of investment return will translate into. In short, it's a succinct "What's *your* (retirement) number?"

The answer to this question will give an idea of the type of retirement we have to look forward to financially. It will also help us to determine what preparatory investment actions we should be prudently taking to get to where we would like to be—the sooner and the more purposefully, the better.

We suggest that as a first step, you find an online retirement calculator in which to input key data. There are plenty available on the Web free of charge; or visit the website of just about any major bank, mutual fund company or investment house you care to choose. There's also your financial advisor. All offer or can provide you with online financial calculators that are easy to use. Input your responses to questions such as:

- When do I plan to retire?
- By how much do I expect my annual income to grow over my remaining working life?
- What do I estimate my annual living expenses to likely be over this period?
- How will my annual pension contributions add up? Do I intend to contribute the statutory annual maximum to my RRSP (incrementally if I belong to a company pension plan, fully if I don't)?

And, best assisted by your financial advisor, answer questions such as:

- What average annual rate of inflation should be assumed?
- What rate of return might I realistically expect on a properly-balanced, risk-weighted portfolio both up to and in retirement?

Now push the button to find out what your accumulated retirement nest egg will need to be and hey, presto! You could well end up staring at your screen in stunned disbelief.

INCREDIBLE? MAYBE NOT

Simple rules of thumb will corroborate that this seemingly incredible number is indeed in the ballpark. In an accompaniment to an excellent article "The Number" by Lee Eisenberg, in *Fortune* on July 12, 2004, it was estimated that to stop work at 65 and live to 90 you would need to multiply your current income by 40 if you are 30 years or younger; by 30 if you're between 40 and 49; and by 25 if you are 50 or older.

Despite your dazed reaction, remember this target number is in future dollars and that compounding can be very powerful. Then go do the math and start feeling better, also more determined.

Thus, if your retirement portfolio earned a reinvestable 6% annually, it would double in 12 years; if 8%, then over nine years; if 10%, in a little over seven years. Add permissible RRSP contributions, determine how much you can add annually to your non-registered portfolio in cash terms, and you could well find your Number becoming a much less stomach-churning proposition.

On the other hand, if your estimates of what you can realistically invest in the time frame available to you keep coming up short, you'll have to consider alternatives to close the retirement gap and remove the worry of your retirement chart showing your portfolio being exhausted way too early.

One such alternative might be to weigh your portfolio(s) more heavily with equities than you would otherwise have liked, perhaps even 100% in equities for their prospective higher-risk returns. If this risk is judged excessive given your personal circumstances and resources, another alternative might be to cut back on your retirement lifestyle expectations; for example, to face the reality you will have to get by on a pro rata 80% or 60% or 50% (rather than 100%) of your pre-retirement income. Or, the taller your retirement order remains, that you will need to work that many years longer, or plan on part-time work in retirement, e.g., doctors doing locums, business people taking on consultancy assignments.

"WAITERS"

While there is no single correct answer or perfect benchmark, and while your Number will depend on how you choose and can afford to live, the worst of all worlds is surely to have no answer at all to what you might need in retirement. Or to join that new class of citizens dubbed "waiters" by Barry Fish and Leslie Kotzer in their self-published book, *The Family Fight: Planning to Avoid It*—made up of financially unsuccessful people waiting for their parents to die so they can get "their share" of an unknown and possibly disputed inheritance. Or to depend on government or your children's largesse.

The answer may not be comforting when you go through what should be a mandatory retirement exercise for all of us. Nevertheless, we can vouch for the fact that you will feel better for it afterwards. It's likely you will also be heartened by what can be done, and the positive adjustments that could be in store once your retirement investment plan develops some self-generating, upside momentum.

In going about an exercise like this to settle on the number—or range of numbers—that's best for you, the younger you are and the sooner you begin a serious personalized investment plan, the better. The older you are and the later you begin, the less likely you'll achieve that desired retirement nest egg, and the higher the retirement sacrifices you are going to have to make. Time waits for no one, most definitely not in an exercise like this. What's *your* Number?

LET ME BE FRANK...

Frank is 38 years old, single and earning $85,000 per year. He is self-employed, and as such has no company pension plan. His pension plan is his RRSP, which is presently valued at $300,000. Frank would like to retire at age 60, and live on 75% of his present income so that he can indulge in his passion for visiting the world's wine regions and sampling their wares. He is able to contribute an average of $15,000 per year to his RRSP.

We begin the process of getting Frank's Number by figuring out what 75% of his present income will be 23 years from now. We've assumed an average annual rate of inflation of 2%. Using this assumption, Frank will be hoping to receive an income of $100,527 in his 60th year, growing this sum by 2% each year to offset the effects of inflation.

We've now solved the first part of the puzzle. We know that Frank has to have enough capital by age 60 to support an income of $100,000 (we're all friends here, so let's round off the numbers), indexed by 2% per annum. How much capital will be needed to generate that income stream for what could be 30 years or more? Breathe deep—it's $2.17 million. And remember, today's generation is more active in retirement and is generally living longer than the generation that preceded it. We may be shortchanging Frank by assuming just 30 years.

Using Frank's current RRSP balance of $300,000, and assuming that he will continue to make contributions of $15,000 per year, growing at 2%, we must find out what average annual compounded rate of return Frank will need to earn on his assets to have him sipping syrah in Sydney. The math shows that if Frank were to earn an average annual compounded rate of return of 6.5% on his money, he should have no trouble in amassing the $2.17 million he will need to fund his retirement lifestyle needs.

Now that Frank has his Number in percentage terms, 6.5%, he can set out to develop an asset allocation strategy that will offer him the greatest prospect of achieving it consistently. The beauty of this method is that if Frank can manage to tune out the distractions of the market, he will be far less prone to making irrational investment decisions. He will know specifically what he must earn to meet his objectives. Every decision he makes will be focused on protecting what he has earned so far, and on achieving his target.

But what if the calculations came back with a required growth rate that simply does not square with historic experience? What if the number was 12% or 15%? This is where a responsible professional can offer a cool, rational point of view. A reliable advisor will point out that generating annual returns in the low to mid-teens with great regularity is a pretty tall order, particularly when we find ourselves in an era of relatively low inflation and low interest rates. If this were the case, we would ask Frank to consider his options.

- Could he work until age 65 instead of 60?
- Is he willing or able to contribute more capital each year than he is at present?
- Could he live on less than the desired 75%?
- Would he consider supplementing his retirement income with occasional consulting work?

Changing the assumptions ever so slightly, particularly when lengthy periods of time are available, can affect the outcome considerably—and often comfortingly.

BENCHMARKS

Once you've got your Number and battened down the required average annual return to reach it, the focus switches to relative performance. This is where an investor makes a comparison between his or her portfolio (or specific components of the portfolio) and one or more of the dozens of benchmark indexes to choose from.

Take a look through your portfolio, gaining a sense of where you have the most representation. If your portfolio is primarily composed of Canadian large-capitalization stocks (either through direct ownership or through the indirect ownership of a mutual fund or other manager-run investment product) then the S&P/TSX Composite Index is probably a good benchmark. If bonds take up much of the available space in your portfolio, then the Scotia Capital Bond Universe is a more appropriate measuring stick.

Apples to Apples

Regardless of which benchmark indexes you use to measure against the performance of your portfolio, make sure they reflect the investments contained within your portfolio. What you are seeking to avoid is a comparison of apples and oranges. You want, to the greatest degree possible, to be making apples to apples comparisons.

Beat the Street

It's only natural for most investors to want to beat the market, thereby attaining or exceeding their targeted number that much more readily. There is no shortage of investment books, articles, seminars and studies on the subject. The fact of the matter is that only a precious few managers consistently outperform the "street" (market index) on a consistent basis. More often than not, this is because the quest to beat the market when indexes are on the rise requires taking on increasing quantities of risk to produce ever-greater investment returns. Eventually, the heightened risk catches up with the investor in a boom-to-bust scenario.

Upside and Downside Participation

The more sensible approach, in our opinion, is to focus on achieving your best relative performance versus an index when that index is going through a period of decline. By doing so, you will likely be committing much of your energies to risk management, an often overlooked aspect of investment management. This is what is known in the investment management field as downside participation. What about rising markets? Set your sights on achieving a percentage of a market's gain. This is what is known as (you guessed it) upside participation.

Performance Expectation Guidelines

We recommend that investors set guidelines for their performance expectations. Many of Bryan's clients are either already retired or are coming very close to the time when they will be able to do so. For this reason, it is not unusual for them to have investment plans that call for upside participation to be somewhere between two-thirds and three-quarters of the gain in a specific benchmark. During periods of market decline, these same investment plans call for downside participation of anywhere between an eighth to a fifth of the benchmark's decline.

Portfolio Performance on a Relative Basis Using the S&P/TSX Composite Index as a Benchmark

	Rising Market Performance	Falling Market Performance
Portfolio	9.3%	(1.7%)
TSX Composite	13.7%	(11.8%)
% Upside/Downside Participation	68%	15%

By taking this approach, you are much less likely to fall into the trap of rushing to pass judgment on the state of your portfolio, resulting in rash investment decisions.

Widely-Used Benchmarks

This is by no means a complete listing of all of the relevant benchmark indexes that investors can use to evaluate the performance of their portfolios. There are

countless sub-indexes that follow industry groups. These permit an investor to
have the ability to compare the performance of a stock or sector-specific mutual
fund against their counterparts. An example would be to compare the performance
of Suncor Energy against the performance of the S&P/TSX Oil & Gas Sub-Index
over a specified time frame.

We won't waste your time by cramming this book full of filler by giving you a
tidy little description of every big-name index out there. The point of the exercise
is to give you an understanding of the big North American, global and international
stock indexes in order to get you started. You own a Japanese mutual fund? Then
do an Internet search on the Nikkei 225 or the Topix. A European fund? Go to the
Dow Jones website and have a look at the Dow Jones Euro STOXX index. Your
fund company and/or your advisor should be able to give you some insights into
what are appropriate benchmarks for your portfolio.

S&P/TSX Composite: This is the most widely followed benchmark index for
stocks in Canada. The index is run by Standard & Poor's, and represents up to 300
of the largest publicly-traded companies. The S&P/TSX Composite is a market-
weighted index, which means value can be heavily impacted by the performance of
the stocks that it tracks. For example, in the halcyon spring of 2000, a high-flying
Nortel rose to represent some 30% of the index. Today, oil stocks and their related
sub-index account for close to one quarter of the index. Therefore, the index
needs to be treated with some caution. Index investing proponents frequently
treat a given index as the ideal representation of the market. Often these people
ignore the natural distortions that can occur within an index.

Dow Jones Industrial Average: Commonly referred to as simply "the Dow,"
this index is the most famous and widely-known of all stock indexes. Composed
of 30 large, well-established American corporations that are widely considered
to be among the leaders in their respective industries, the Dow is what is known
as a price-weighted index. This is viewed by some as a key disadvantage because
it means that a stock that trades at $100 but has a market capitalization of $1
billion (the number of shares outstanding multiplied by the share price) will
receive a bigger weighting in the index than a stock that trades at $50 yet has a
market capitalization of $5 billion. It is because of the price weighting and the
representation of just 30 stocks that the Dow is dismissed by some critics as not
being a fair representation of the whole market.

Standard & Poor's 500: This is the index most often cited by professionals as the best benchmark for U.S. stocks. As the name implies, it tracks 500 companies chosen for their market size, liquidity and sector. While there are some mid-sized companies in the index, most are considered to be large-capitalization companies. The S&P 500 is a market-weighted index.

NASDAQ Composite: This index tracks all of the stocks listed on the NASDAQ exchange. Because so many so-called "new economy" companies are listed on the NASDAQ, this composite index is considered a heart rate monitor of sorts for the over 5,000 largely technology stocks listed on this exchange. Though this makes the NASDAQ Composite a useful tool for gaining an expansive view of the market, critics claim that the index is composed of far too many small, illiquid stocks. The performance of these small names can sometimes be quite volatile, making the index itself more volatile than would otherwise be the case.

MSCI World: For a snapshot of how the global capital markets are performing, many professional investors turn to the MSCI World Index. This market-weighted index is a benchmark for large, publicly traded companies in approximately 150 countries around the world. It is frequently used as a benchmark for comparing the performance of many global mutual funds.

MSCI EAFE: The primary difference between this index and the MSCI World Index is the EAFE (Europe, Australia and Far East) constraint, which means that the MSCI EAFE Index omits stocks that are listed in emerging markets and in North America. Twenty-one individual country indexes are represented in this index, which is typically used as a benchmark for international funds. International funds differ from global funds in that a global fund manager normally must invest just about anywhere in the developed world. This compares with an international fund manager, who must usually invest anywhere in the developed world with the exception of North America. The MSCI EAFE Index is a market-weighted index.

ABSOLUTE VS. RELATIVE RETURNS

In his groundbreaking 2004 book on investing entitled *Bull's Eye Investing*, author John Mauldin builds his case for the need to seek out consistent absolute returns rather than striving to achieve relative returns.

Absolute or Relative

Absolute Return: The rate of return on a specific investment or investment portfolio, taken as a stand-alone number. Absolute returns are usually compared against a target return that an investor has stated as their desired investment performance. (Please see Chapter 12 for more information on benchmarking performance.)

Relative Return: The rate of return that an investor has achieved relative to a specific market index. For example, if the S&P/TSX Composite Index is down 10% in a given year, but an investor's portfolio is down by 2% over that same time period, that portfolio will be considered to have delivered a superior relative return.

Mauldin believes that for the foreseeable future, the world's capital markets will fail to match the kind of wealth-building growth that typified the 1980s and 1990s. His main reason for thinking this way is the demographic trends that have the baby boomer generation rapidly approaching retirement over the next 10 to 15 years. Approaching and safely achieving retirement is when the demand and need for consistent investment gains is of greatest importance for any investor. It is precisely for this reason that Mauldin urges his readers to focus on absolute return strategies such as those found among alternative investment managers.

Mauldin's reasoning is entirely understandable. As retirement draws nearer, the need for consistency in terms of investment performance grows. Swinging for the fences with each appearance at home plate brings an above-average probability of strikeouts. For a young investor, with many years of working for a livelihood and portfolio contributions ahead, temporary setbacks as the result of a financial strikeout can be repaired over time. However, that same luxury is not available to the investor approaching retirement. Far better to advance the runners on base, in our view, than to risk an "out" if retirement is five years or less away.

YOU'VE GOT THE DESTINATION, NOW GET A MAP

Instead of flying blind, that worst of all worlds, you should have your own road map to retirement. Tools, like the MapQuest program that helped guide Michael to Borsheim's (a trip you'll learn about in the next chapter) are readily available and simple to use. Once you have arrived at your Number, you and your financial advisor can map out your journey using an Investment Policy Statement or equivalent investment plan as a guide. That document is where everything we've described in *Portfolio First Aid* will begin coming together in a cohesive plan. We'll explore what needs to go into a carefully crafted Investment Policy Statement in the next chapter. And how, once it is implemented, occasional road closures and detours will never push you off your intended course.

Best of all, by going about it this way you will have considerably reduced—if not eliminated—the risk of your and/or your spouse living to 90 and having to ask your kids for cash. Chances are, knowing your Number will also bring you the quiet confidence from which carefully considered investment decisions flow.

CHAPTER 13

The Roadmap to Peace—
and Prosperity

Investment Policy Statements

Late afternoon, Friday, April 29, 2005: Just as he had every spring for the past 12 years, Michael made the journey—a pilgrimage of sorts—to Omaha for the annual meeting of the shareholders of Berkshire Hathaway. For three days, Buffett devotees of all ages and from around the world gathered in what has come to be known as "the Woodstock of Capitalism." Michael's long-time friend, Jim Springer, who usually drives from Arizona to join him for the annual meeting, couldn't come this year. Jim usually acted as chauffeur during their stay in Omaha, so his absence meant that Michael would have to rent a car and drive himself to the Berkshire Hathaway annual shareholders' reception at Borsheim's, an upscale jewellery store in the suburbs of this pleasant but spread-out heartland city. Michael had been to these receptions enough to roughly know the way, and he might have been able to get there on his own, but maybe not. The commonsensical solution: provide MapQuest with the necessary coordinates (specifically, where he was starting from and finishing at) and request the trip plan summarized in the box below.

Airport Ramada to Borsheim's	
WEST on E. LOCUST ST.	0.1 km
Turn LEFT onto ABBOTT DR.	2.7 km
ABBOTT DR. becomes CUMING ST.	0.5 km
Turn LEFT onto N. 16th ST.	0.6 km
Turn RIGHT onto CHICAGO ST.	0.1 km
Turn RIGHT onto ramp	0.5 km
Merge onto I-480 W	4.1 km
Merge onto I-80 W via Exit 452C	11.0 km
Merge onto I-680 N via Exit 446	4.0 km
Take US-6/W. DODGE ROAD Exit 3	0.4 km
Merge onto W. DODGE ROAD /US-6E	0.9 km
Take REGENCY PKWY ramp toward 96th-102nd Sts.	0.1 km
Merge onto REGENCY PKWY	0.4 km
End at 120 Regency Pkwy	

Estimated: Time 22 minutes; Distance 25.4 kilometres

Even with the detailed directions from MapQuest, the trip to Borsheim's turned out to be a journey with lots of challenging manoeuvres. With guest navigator Neil Hamilton reading the directions, Michael duly reached the reception, but not without an unexpected wrong turn caused by a road-construction diversion, arriving about 20 minutes later than scheduled.

Realistically, Michael wouldn't have been able to reach his intended destination at all without the help of a well-laid-out plan. It's the same in successful investing, just that the targets are different.

SET THE COORDINATES

Replace the departure point and arrival destination in this example with where you are currently in terms of your finances and where you will need to be at some set time in the future to be able to adequately provide the capital to meet stated objectives. Instead of minutes and miles, substitute years and financial contributions for the attainment of those all-important goals. A serious, thoughtful approach to investing is guided by a set of clearly articulated objectives set out in advance by the investor. This should always be the starting point in the drafting of an Investment Policy Statement (IPS).

Just as the trip to Borsheim's on that late-April afternoon required careful, en route adjustments, so too does the launching and nurturing of a well-planned investment portfolio designed to serve as the vehicle to reach a long-term destination such as a financially independent retirement. This preliminary step in laying out an Investment Policy Statement can easily be summarized in a statement worthy of the Yankee great Yogi Berra: You'll never get to where you're going if you don't know where you're going to.

THE TRINITY

That all-important Number described in the previous chapter may be representative of the investor's goal(s), but a careful plan needs to be drawn up for how to achieve it. The execution of this plan needs to be measured and accounted for along the way. The successful investing trinity includes three essentials that should function in unison:

- ongoing performance benchmarks
- accountability
- the investment policy statement to tie it all together

Every investment relationship must begin with the prospective client supplying basic information about himself or herself: full name, address, date of birth, social insurance number, employment information, marital status, family particulars and the type of investment account(s) needing to be opened. The investment industry's mandatory Know Your Client (KYC) form also requires the disclosure of salient information about net worth (annual income, assets and liabilities), the level of risk to be run (high, medium, low), the objectives (short-, medium- and long-term; capital gains and/or income), previous investment experience (in stocks, bonds, mutual funds, etc.) and the knowledge of investing (sophisticated, limited, average, none). While the KYC document is a useful starting point, it is not enough by itself. A truly successful client-advisor relationship needs a lot more.

Opening an investment account is an undertaking in which the clearer the paper trail, the better. To get things properly understood and started, for *en passant* reference and, heaven forbid, in case there are future disputes, clarify in writing even the most basic of investment needs.

Many advisors are happy to work off the KYC form. Others will also make their own notes during the initial interview and any further meetings to set up the account. Some like filling in more expansive questionnaires (for example, an estate planning questionnaire) to record the facts and understanding they will need. There will usually be follow-up letters summarizing what is planned. Some advisors make a point of taking new clients through their first few monthly account statements line by line. Some firms like to go through the paperwork page by page on the signing of an engagement agreement with a new client. Regardless of how it is done, have something down on paper to go by. Setting down agreed-upon points in writing at the outset can go a long way toward avoiding potentially costly and damaging disagreements later on.

In a perfect world, simple point-form notes kept in your client file to record the minutes of your meetings would suffice. In a perfect world there would be no misunderstandings. Neither would there be any forgetfulness. Investment decisions would be devoid of emotion. Banquet burgers would be considered health food and everyone's children would have above-average intelligence. Let's get our heads out of the clouds and remember that the world we live in is full of imperfection. In the real world, what is required and agreed upon should be recorded in an Investment Policy Statement (IPS).

CHARTING YOUR COURSE: ESSENTIAL ELEMENTS OF THE INVESTMENT POLICY STATEMENT

A carefully crafted IPS takes the documentation process one giant leap beyond the basic outline of assets, liabilities and risk tolerance found within the Know Your Client form. A sound IPS addresses four basic elements:

1. quantifying and time-bounding the investment objectives
2. defining the asset allocation policy
3. setting out management procedures (dos and don'ts for the portfolio manager)
4. delineating performance benchmarks and the frequency of performance reporting (monthly, quarterly or semi-annually)

With an IPS, an investor can expect a document that clearly outlines what is expected from their investment portfolio and guidelines on what steps the advisor/portfolio manager, etc., can and cannot take in the management of the portfolio. An example of this is in the minimum acceptable credit quality for fixed-income securities in the portfolio. A risk-averse client may have his or her IPS declare that fixed-income investments must carry a credit rating of single "A" or better.

An IPS is designed to map out in careful detail the investment goals and the measures and procedures needed to attain them. According to the Canadian Securities Institute's textbook on *Portfolio Management Techniques*, the role of the IPS is to "clearly state the client's objectives and constraints, as well as to detail the tools and strategies available to the manager to meet the client's objectives, subject to the client's constraints." Familiarity with Investment Policy Statements is also a vital component of the Chartered Financial Analyst (CFA) qualification, with CFA candidates even asked to memorize that they consist of two primary factors: objectives and constraints. The objectives are risk and return; the constraints are time frame, degree of accompanying liquidity, taxes, legal and regulatory requirements, and unique needs.

Documentation like this is usually required in precise detail at the pension fund and institutional levels and also is often a legal necessity. For example, the IPS for the University of California General Endowment Pool runs to 60 pages, in which investment goals and policies, fiduciary oversight procedures, performance objectives, and asset class and manager guidelines are spelled out in copious detail and are supported by exhaustive appendices.

While preparation like this needn't be nearly as onerous at the individual investor level, a good IPS will bring necessary discipline to both client and advisor—even more so if it is written in clearly understandable language (as opposed to "legalese"). It will help to keep emotions in check through periods of market turbulence. Clients and their advisors will find they are better able to coexist and work together through tough times.

Define the Asset Allocation Policy

Now that your objectives have been clarified and quantified, the next stage in creating a workable Investment Policy Statement is to spell out the asset allocation that will strike the balance between risk and return on an ongoing basis. Imbedded as part of this stage are guidelines as to when and how the advisor should rebalance the portfolio. Be careful here to allow your advisor enough latitude so that he or she will not be compelled to prematurely cut short winning positions. Similarly, a good asset allocation policy will set out minimum weightings for certain asset classes.

Here is an example of an asset allocation policy that Bryan set down for one of his clients a few years ago:

- cash and equivalents: 5%–15%
- high-yield bonds: 0%–5%
- investment-grade bonds: 20%–35%
- income trusts and REITs: 15%–20%
- small-cap Canadian equities: 5%–10%
- mid-cap Canadian equities: 10%–15%
- large-cap Canadian equities: 25%–35%
- large-cap American equities: 15%–25%

From the above holding limits, it is then possible to recommend a portfolio. One possible portfolio that could have been initially constructed from these limits is below.

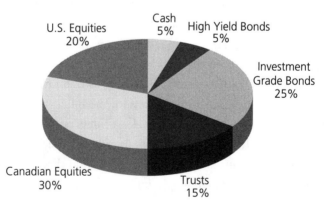

Under New Management

From an advisor's perspective, the heart of the IPS is the section that concerns the selection, monitoring and evaluation of the performance of the investments making their way into the portfolio. The same three elements (selection, monitoring and evaluation) can be used for situations where third-party investment managers have been utilized to manage a portfolio. This is another prime example of where planning ahead and putting agreed-upon points in writing will make life a lot less acrimonious for everyone concerned when markets become troublesome.

Just as constraints are placed in the asset allocation section on how much or how little representation each particular asset class should have in the portfolio, so too should there be clearly documented constraints on the inclusion or exclusion of certain types of investments, industry categories or geographic representations. As a matter of ethical concern, for example, an investor may not wish to have any tobacco-related stocks in his or her portfolio.

This section of the IPS can also be used to state what the minimum acceptable credit quality is for a fixed-income investment to make its way into the portfolio.

We Need to Talk

We have stated many times throughout this book that one of the most frequent causes of a breakdown in the relationship between an advisor and a client is poor communication. This can come in many forms, from regular conversations that fail to get to the heart of the matter to long periods where the advisor and client are entirely out of communication, which often result in pressing yet unresolved issues. The IPS should address the issue of communication clearly. It should spell out how often the client and the advisor are going to sit down to discuss the progress of the portfolio. The client should know in advance what will be covered in these meetings because it will be spelled out clearly in the IPS.

Investment Policy Statements (or their equivalent) should also be regarded as dynamic documents not to be locked away and forgotten. Instead, they should be kept handy for regular reference and for adjustment when investor needs and market conditions change, as they do from time to time. Whatever the form of documentation, carefully recording the relationship between investor and advisor can only facilitate the investment process to follow.

BENCHMARKING PERFORMANCE: MILESTONES ALONG THE ROAD

Hand in hand with the road map and the launching of the portfolio are the benchmarks, or milestones, that will be needed to measure how the "journey" is progressing. It is through the selection of these milestones that you and your advisor will be able to determine whether your portfolio is on or off course to achieve planned targets and what, if any, course corrections should be made.

Every serious investor wants to know how his or her portfolio is faring relative to the markets as a whole, as well as to other comparable portfolios and/or similarly structured mutual funds. It's not hard to measure the latest monthly statements against those of earlier periods. A comparison of the most recent portfolio total with earlier totals will provide the appreciation or depreciation over the period being measured (adjusted for any deposits or withdrawals). Add to this, the investment income that has been received divided by the average value of the portfolio over the period to obtain the yield. Then add the two together and you will have the total return to compare with your plan and also for comparison with the returns on corresponding benchmarks.

An exercise like this is best done over a calendar year or the preceding 12 months for an annualized return to compare with others. The market benchmarks are usually readily available in the financial press or from your advisor. If your portfolio is balanced between equities and fixed income, you'll want to average the overall market returns to see how your return compares. If, for example, yours is a portfolio balanced evenly between equities and fixed income, and the total annual returns on related market indexes were 15% and 7% respectively (as was the case in the Canadian markets in 2004), then your benchmark return against which to compare would be 11%. If your portfolio's return is superior, good; if it is in line, okay. Ask pointed questions if it is lower.

Distant Early Warning

You should be prepared to give your portfolio and your advisor a reasonable amount of time to do the expected job. We prefer to measure account performance over four continuously moving periods—five years, three years, one year and three months. These measurements are then compared with the markets as a whole, and also against a comparable universe of mutual funds, principally equity and balanced funds. What really counts in an exercise like this are the relative performance rankings over five years and three years, periods long enough to include market ups and downs (maybe even a change from bull to bear, or bear to bull). This gives an advisor or a portfolio manager ample opportunity to show their mettle. This is not to say that you need to wait three years before passing judgment on the work of your advisor. Just as making dramatic transformations to the composition of your portfolio after a week or a month would be ludicrous, so too would be waiting an extended period of time before taking action to rectify a portfolio that is failing to meet reasonable expectations. We recommend that you use a rolling 12-month period as your distant early warning system.

ACCOUNTABILITY

Accountability is the third leg of the proverbial stool that is an effective investment policy statement. It's an old term that takes on fresh meaning as new and improved measuring tools are developed. Evidence of this is seen in the latest reporting systems, which are enabling advisors to provide their clients with easy-to-understand performance-related information at the click of a button.

The numbers tell only part of the story, though. Analysis of the performance and the portfolio over specified periods of time by someone possessing both experience and expertise will inevitably be necessary to keep your portfolio from straying too far off course. Examples of good analysis are evident in statements such as:

- "Your portfolio performance fell short because we didn't have enough representation in oils and financials, a misjudgment on my (the advisor's) part; I will need to do something about this."
- "You didn't do as well as the market benchmarks because we held excessive cash reserves earning less than 2%, and Canadian equities gathered surprising momentum to average returns of 15%. My future challenge will be to deploy this excessive cash to make up the lost ground."
- "We didn't do as well as the market benchmarks because they were heavily driven by soaring oil stocks, which we had agreed were too risky for your more conservative, income-driven portfolio, where the emphasis is on utilities and dividend-paying equities."
- "Do you remember that 'hot' stock you insisted I buy for you in a large quantity? It subsequently plummeted, pulling down your portfolio's return by 2%."
- "Look at the difference made by that major withdrawal from your portfolio, which forced me to liquidate (sell) holdings I would have otherwise kept."
- "Look how much better you compare when all your family's accounts are consolidated and we have a total picture for you and your spouse."

The markets are dynamic by nature. Course corrections are an inescapable inevitability. This is why we believe it is imperative that the frequency and terms of performance reporting and communication, personified by accountability, plays an integral role in the drafting of a worthwhile IPS.

In the final instance, investing must always involve the unpredictable and the unforeseen; that is, the running of risk in return for prospective reward. What a difference if performance can be realistically measured and progressively accounted for. You can hold your advisor fully accountable, but you must be accountable too. This way, one plus one will add up to considerably more than two.

FACILITATING OWNER-PARTNERSHIP

At the annual meeting the day after the reception that Michael needed professional help to get to, Messrs. Buffett and Munger gave over 20,000 Berkshire Hathaway shareholders and their guests a memorable six-hour lesson in owner-partnership, which is what they believe successful investing should be all about. Warren and Charlie love the idea of shareholders thinking and behaving like owners.

Near-term earnings and share price fluctuations don't matter to them, but results over a long period of time do. The Berkshire record speaks for itself. Between their takeover of Berkshire Hathaway in 1965 and the end of 2004, book value grew from $19 to $55,824 per Class "A" share, a rate of 21.9% compounded annually. In addition, the annual growth in per share book value—their best benchmark for measuring the long-term rate of increase in Berkshire's intrinsic (i.e., true) value—exceeded the annual return on the S&P 500 Index (dividends included) in 34 of these 40 years. Some roadmap, some benchmarks! The accountability to their shareholders, i.e., their owner-partners, couldn't be more transparent or understandable. They are rightfully proud of their disciplined yet simple recipe for success. If these consummate value investors can use roadmaps and benchmarks so successfully, we should at the very least want to equip ourselves similarly. Accountability would then take on an added meaning for us as well.

AS TIME GOES BY

Just as Michael's trip to Borsheim's was fraught with unexpected detours, so too will be your financial journey. A good roadmap, represented by a personalized and thorough Investment Policy Statement, will help ensure that you reach your intended destination safely and on time. The process itself of drafting an Investment Policy Statement is one that will strengthen the bond between you and your advisor, permitting the advisor to understand both your wants and needs on a deeper level than would otherwise be the case. Putting the outcome of these initial discussions into a written, time-bounded format will go a long way to ensuring that there is less room for misunderstanding or disagreement as time goes by.

CHAPTER 14

Connecting the Dots

We set the background for *Portfolio First Aid* in the fear-filled summer of 1982; we conclude our treatise on healthier investing in the jittery summer of 2005. What a roller coaster ride in between! We've traced how investors endured, and what they needed to do to survive one of the most tumultuous periods in stock market history—a period that featured extremes in pessimism and exuberance, leading to nerve-testing market volatility. Over these years we've also had the most spectacular bull market in history and among the most savage bear markets of all time. Seldom have investors ever been put to the test against extremes like these.

As the markets continued their relentless upward trajectory in the 1990s and on into a Y2K-free new millennium, investors and their advisors showed increasing overconfidence. Few dared to foresee the financial blood-letting that would follow, let alone take precautionary provisions in their investment planning. This became the genesis for *Portfolio First Aid*: to diagnose the ailments that have afflicted so many portfolios, to prescribe necessary remedies and to engage in a fitness regimen for lasting financial health.

We are enormously confident that the path to the quality of life you dream of for yourself and your heirs runs through today's global capital markets. Remember the time-honoured adage about the trend being the investor's friend. The trends all around us are highly encouraging. Increasingly, too, they are democratically based and market-driven. The year 2004 marked the first time that more than half the world's population voted for the government of their choosing. As democracy spreads, so will the accompanying investment opportunities.

The decades since World War II have brought breathtaking lifestyle changes and technological advancement that were scarcely imaginable when the Cold War began in the late-1940s, even when it ended in the early-1990s. Hand in hand has gone ever-lengthening life expectancy. Prosperity and opportunity for investment wealth accumulation keep gathering momentum as the march of progress continues. Truly, the trends continue to be the investor's friend.

That's the good news. The bad news is that as opportunities lead to newfound prosperity, risk is magnified. It's a dual-edged sword that all investors must contend with. And it's precisely because of today's enhanced opportunities and commensurate risks that more investors will, from time to time, need portfolio first aid to soothe the financial bumps and scrapes along the way. It's a situation that is somewhat analogous to the proliferation of sports-injury clinics as people become more active well into, and often beyond, middle age.

> *"Markets can remain irrational longer than you can remain solvent."*
> John Maynard Keynes

The legendary Lord Keynes's dour yet apt observation about markets' irrational staying power is a sobering reminder of the need to temper optimism with prudence. Even at the best of times, risk is the investor's constant companion. The irrationality Keynes speaks of only makes it an even more difficult beast to tame. Even when markets reach dizzying heights, risk is always lurking nearby. Being constantly conscious of risk—and how to handle it—ranks among the most valuable lessons we hope to leave with you.

A FORCE OF NATURE

This doesn't mean one should take a fatalistic approach to risk. Instead, it gets us to another primary purpose of *Portfolio First Aid*: namely, to remind our readership that in investing there is nothing new under the sun. Expect irrationality and be prepared to confront it head on. It may be trite to say this, but we want you to prepare for the worst and hope for the best, staying financially healthy in the process. Remember, we are enthusiastic believers in the long-term viability of the capital markets provided we as investors treat market forces, which are in many respects like forces of nature, with care and respect.

QUALITY IS NEVER AN ACCIDENT

Michael's personal trainer, Daryl Devonish, has a favourite catchphrase: "Quality is never an accident." His belief is that a better quality of life is something we should work to make happen through exercise and a healthy lifestyle over many years. Daryl has also drilled the single word "focus" into Michael's psyche. He directs Michael to focus not only on the hour with him, but also on the next exercise to the exclusion of everything else in order to achieve the desired result.

Quality of life is investment-related too, even more so if the successful deployment of your investment savings brings accompanying peace of mind. Your investment success shouldn't be left to chance, even if on occasion the markets take on the appearance of a giant casino. Success in the competitive marketplace is seldom an accident.

Professional athletes, artists and musicians can make their challenges appear simple. However, the mastery of their craft doesn't happen without sacrifice. What they do with seeming effortlessness is the result of endless patience, dedication and determination, far from the roar of the crowd. Success in the arena that is the world's financial markets requires the same qualities as those of the virtuoso musician and the champion athlete. Just think of Warren Buffett and John Templeton to appreciate what we mean. Why not also everyday investors? Never forget that exceptional performance comes as a result of persistence and discipline, never dumb luck.

We're not so naive as to think that there won't be a fair share of cuts and bruises along the way. Everyone, including your authors, has the battle scars to prove it. Instead, in *Portfolio First Aid* we've tried to point the way to a more consistently successful portfolio and to equip you with the knowledge to deal with the inevitable setbacks as you remain focused on attaining well-planned investment goals.

If this book has had one central theme it is that *your* investing should be all about *you*. It's *your* money, and you are the one who has to make the key investment decisions that will ultimately dictate the standard of living *you* wish to enjoy later in life. Furthermore, it's up to you whether you choose to handle your investing yourself, or to enlist the help of others. Of course, we're more than a little biased on the subject. Having said that, we advise the latter because of the many ways simple investment fundamentals can become complicated by cross-currents of emotion and rapidly changing circumstances.

Those who are not prepared to commit the requisite time and patience to their investing can very easily become overwhelmed. For many individual investors, going it alone is a far too daunting task, comparable to running a solo marathon. Having a reliable, trusted advisor by your side to exercise dispassionate reason at those critical junctures when emotion overcomes logic can save you many times what you may have to pay in fees or commissions.

Warren Buffett and his partner, Charlie Munger, have their famed intrinsic value approach. We like the value approach too, through which we assess what a company should be worth, compare our assessment with the prevailing market price of its shares and tailor our investment recommendation accordingly. It's an approach reinforced by a strong investment discipline and designed to achieve superior long-term returns at below-average risk.

Other investment managers also have their own distinctive styles. The combinations and permutations of investment methodologies are almost limitless. The important thing to remember is that the whole process—whatever that may entail—should be focused *on you*. Above all, pick the style and strategy of an advisor/investment manager that speaks to *your* needs.

EARLY DETECTION

Study after study has shown that the key to survival with many once-incurable diseases is early detection. Scores of men are now screened regularly for prostate cancer and an even greater number of women are regularly checked for early signs of breast cancer. The net result is a greatly improved rate of detection and survival. A similar situation exists regarding the long-term state of its health. Early detection through the careful measurement of its performance against pre-selected benchmarks will go a long way to helping you identify and respond to trouble before it can cause permanent damage to your financial well-being.

To be a long-term investor is, by definition, to be an optimist. On that score, we both stand guilty as charged. Our final piece of advice for you is to take lessons from the past, but always look to the future if you wish to be a successful investor. The last several years have brought more than their fair share of challenges and opportunities. Thankfully, the opportunities have outnumbered the challenges, even though at times that seemed highly improbable. We see no reason why the future should be any different.

With *Portfolio First Aid* we've sought to offer you practical advice on how to overcome inevitable setbacks, pushing ahead to meet your goals. We hope we've left you with an exciting picture of investing as it could pertain to you.

YOU AIN'T SEEN NOTHIN' YET!

Al Jolson ushered in a breathtaking new era of communication and technological evolution when he spoke the first words in a "talkie." Jolson's words marked a permanent step forward, not just for the motion picture industry but for the transference of information around the world. Today, almost a century later, technological evolution is still helping change the world. Opportunities are opening up in more ways and for more people than at any other time in human history. We should want to be stakeholders. There is surely no better way to participate in the evolutionary progress of humankind than as investors.

As previously, in the summer of 1975, Benjamin Graham adapted a quote from Virgil to describe investors as "enviably" fortunate. In a similar vein, we'll conclude by paraphrasing Al Jolson's famous line to emphasize our optimism regarding future prospects for today's investors: *You ain't seen nothin' yet!*

Index